The End of Government

Government
. . . as we know it

The End of Government

Government

. . . AS WE KNOW IT

Making Public Policy Work

Elaine C. Kamarck

LYNNE
RIENNER
PUBLISHERS

BOULDER
LONDON

Published in the United States of America in 2007 by
Lynne Rienner Publishers, Inc.
1800 30th Street, Boulder, Colorado 80301
www.rienner.com

and in the United Kingdom by
Lynne Rienner Publishers, Inc.
3 Henrietta Street, Covent Garden, London WC2E 8LU

Library of Congress Cataloging-in-Publication Data
Kamarck, Elaine Ciulla.
The end of government . . . as we know it : making public policy work / Elaine C. Kamarck.
Includes bibliographical references and index.
ISBN-13: 978-1-58826-469-5 (hardcover : alk. paper)
ISBN-13: 978-1-58826-494-7 (pbk. : alk. paper)
1. Administrative agencies—United States—Management. 2. Bureaucracy—United States.
3. Government productivity—United States. I. Title.
JK421.K36 2007
351.73—dc22   2006024835

British Cataloguing in Publication Data
A Cataloguing in Publication record for this book
is available from the British Library.

Printed and bound in the United States of America

The paper used in this publication meets the requirements
of the American National Standard for Permanence of
Paper for Printed Library Materials Z39.48-1992.

5 4 3 2 1

To my father,
Andrew J. Ciulla
(1926–2006),
a great public servant

Contents

Preface

I STILL REMEMBER staring at the telephone. It was one of those big, cream-colored, boxy things with three plastic buttons, one for each line, and a big, red plastic "hold" button. No voice mail, no speaker phone, no conference calling, no automatic redial. I had not seen a phone like that in years.

It was 1993 and my first day on the staff of the new president of the United States, Bill Clinton, and the new vice president, Al Gore. The phone was in the Executive Office of the President—a building within the White House complex and a few hundred yards away from the center of power of the most powerful government in the world. And yet, the phone on my kitchen counter was more sophisticated.

Eventually the White House complex got phones that did what modern ones at that time could do, and we got computers, e-mail, and most of the other things that characterize modern offices. But I still remember that phone. For the full four-and-a-half years I spent there working on reinventing the federal government, every step forward, from closing obsolete agriculture department field offices to passing major procurement legislation to putting government services on the Internet, was greeted with a chorus of complaints from congressional and interest group protectors. As the famous and late management guru Peter Drucker wrote, we were accomplishing things that were remarkable in government, but that would not be so anywhere else. Perhaps that was why, in spite of a series of modest and not-so-modest victories, I never got rid of the nagging suspicion that the government we were trying to reform was like that phone—functioning, but at the same time hopelessly obsolete. We were operating on a corpse, or rearranging the deck chairs on the *Titanic,* or filling the hole in the dike with chewing gum.

You get the picture.

Eight years later, after I had left the government, that feeling came back to haunt me. On September 11, 2001, the United States experienced the largest terrorist attack on its soil in history, and the obsolescence of the government was put into stark relief. Organizations that had defeated the Nazis, the Japanese, and then the Soviet Union were no match for a handful of terrorists. With the attacks on the World Trade Center and the Pentagon, the defense establishment had to face up to the fact that it had been built in another era and was practically impotent in the face of problems of the twenty-first century.

Four Septembers later the government failed once again. When a massive hurricane hit New Orleans, the wealthiest government in the world was caught unaware and unprepared. In the pictures beamed round the world, the US government looked no more competent than one in the third world when it came to protecting the health and welfare of its citizens.

In the coming century we will look to government to fight a war on terror, deal with the potentially powerful emergent economies of China and India, fund the enormous retirement and health care costs of an aging population, and cope with a myriad of unanticipated crises, many of which will be natural. It goes without saying that this will cost a great deal of money. But of equal, if not greater, import is the fact that this will require a government more flexible, more creative, and more able to cope with uncertainty than the government of the twentieth century. This book is dedicated to the topic of policy implementation in this new century. It is a book about the business of government that goes beyond the ends to grapple with the means of government.

The book transcends the tired politics of the left and the right, presenting a new way of governing—one that is more modern, more flexible, and less bureaucratic. It shows how, by looking beyond the bureaucratic option, we can increase the capacity and effectiveness of government in the twenty-first century.

1

The Revolution in Governing

The Bureaucratic Century

Imagine that the year is 1954 and you have to go to the bank to make a deposit, get some cash, and move money between accounts. In 1954 you had to go to a bank between nine o'clock in the morning and three in the afternoon ("banker's hours"). You had to stand in line, see a teller, and have your documents ready. If you were lucky the teller was pleasant to you. Of course, if your bank was the only one in town, your teller did not really have to be nice.

Now imagine that it is 1954 and you have to register your car and renew your passport. You go to an office during the day, probably taking time off from work; you stand in line and have your documents ready; if you are lucky the government official is civil even though there is no reason for such behavior. After all, the government is the ultimate monopoly.

Basically, doing business in the private sector in the early 1950s was not much different than doing so in the public sector.

Now fast forward about half a century. The information revolution had allowed banks to replace many personnel with automatic teller machines (ATMs), and a few years later there was home-based Internet banking. There is no need to go anywhere to check a bank account balance. For instance, a paycheck is deposited automatically, and cash is available at any time of day or night at any handy ATM. People complained about the impersonality of this new world of banking—for about two seconds. But, they quickly became accustomed to the ease and the convenience of banking any time they wanted. As in so many other areas of the consumer world, convenience for the customer became a key to business success and a guide to organizational restructuring.

But this was not so in government. In the public sector in the early 1990s you still had to go to an office, stand in line, and hope that if you got to the head of the line before the office closed you had the right information with you and could in fact complete your business. In 1954 that did not infuriate people as much as forty years later; by 1994 the private sector was changing but the public sector was not. Citizens noticed and complained. Typical of the letters that came to the National Performance Review office in the White House during the Clinton administration was one from Los Angeles. The letter was from an obviously well-to-do man (the first thing he stated was that in the previous year he had paid over $400,000 in federal income taxes). What had made him angry enough to write was his attempt to get his newborn daughter a passport. After he had stood in line for a very long time, the office simply closed—with no apologies to the people who had been waiting. They were simply told to come back the next day. This is an example of how, by the end of the twentieth century, the distance between the private and the public sectors was large and growing, and Americans—along with citizens of other information-age democracies—noticed and complained.

This was not the case for most of the twentieth century, which was in organizational terms the bureaucratic century. In both the public and private sectors, the dominant organizational form was the large, hierarchical, rule-bound entity known as bureaucracy. In the private sector bureaucracy was the analog to the assembly line and the scientific management revolution started by Frederick Taylor. In the public sector, Weberian bureaucracy, with its emphasis on merit and on the separation of person from office, became the preferred mode of getting the government's business done. Like their counterparts in industry, government managers created hierarchical organizations that broke down the complex tasks of government into definable and discrete subtasks, which were then broken into smaller subtasks, and so on.

Twentieth-century government conducted its business through the equivalent of the assembly line. For most of that time, in the United States and other developed countries, the organization structures of the private and public sectors were pretty much the same. The absence of information technology—especially large computers for storing and analyzing data—meant that many organizations, from the Social Security Administration (SSA) to private-sector insurance companies, spent much of their time collecting and organizing records. The employees of these large organizations consisted largely of clerks and their supervisors. A photograph from the Office of Personnel Management in Washington illustrates this better than words ever can (see Photo 1.1). Taken in the middle of the twentieth century, it shows a very large room filled with what seems like hundreds of people, most all of them men, wearing the short haircuts of the day, white shirts, and those skinny dark

(Courtesy of the Office of Personnel Management, Washington, DC)

Photo 1.1   The Census Bureau Mid-Century

ties. The federal government and most state and local governments were, for most of the century, governments of clerks.

But by the end of the twentieth century the private sector was changing the way citizens saw their government. This manifested itself in a paradox. In the world's most advanced democracies, citizens who lived in countries, which had, by many objective measures, done a good job of delivering public goods, were getting evermore critical of their governments.[1] Nowhere was it so apparent as in the United States where, over a period of four decades in which the United States was prosperous and mostly at peace, Americans trusted their government less and less, as Figure 1.1 illustrates.

In an entire book of essays on this topic called *Why People Don't Trust Government* various explanations are tried and found wanting.[2] An examination of this decline reveals that it persisted in the face of changing economic fortunes, it persisted in the face of real governmental accomplishments, and it persisted in the face of changes in political parties and policies.[3] In one of the essays Gary Orren summed up the frus-

Figure 1.1   Trust in Government, 1958–2003 (Percentage responding "Just about always/Most of the time")

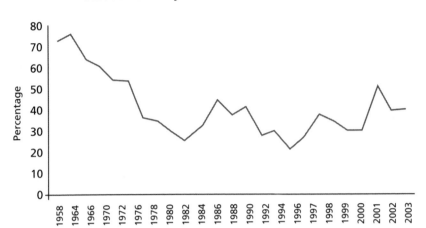

Source: Data from 1958 to 1998, "Pew People and the Press Reports, Questionnaire Part II: How Americans View Government," http://people-press.org/reports; data from 1999–2001, "Hart/Teeter Poll for Council for Excellence in Government, Study # 6446a," p. 7; data from 2002, "Princeton Survey Research Associates for the Brookings Institution," http://www. brookings.edu; data from 2003, CBS/*New York Times* poll, July 11–15, 2004.

tration: "All the usual suspects—those demographic, psychological, social and economic factors that at first seem to offer convenient explanations for declining trust in government—can be dismissed or at least deferred until a more conclusive correlation is proved."[4]

Looking at the persistence of these data across the decades of the late twentieth century and the times' different political situations, it is hard to avoid the conclusion that there was something about government in its form and behavior that made late-twentieth-century Americans angry regardless of government's purpose. Sometime in the late-twentieth century Americans had come to a rather widespread conclusion about the organizations, or means, of government. In short, they hated it. To too many Americans, "government" meant organizations that were large, ponderous, inflexible, and obsolete.

Politicians, not only in the United States, were aware of these sentiments. Ronald Reagan, Brian Mulroney, and Margaret Thatcher made impressive careers out of such dissatisfaction.[5] Stories of stupid government fueled not only conservative political revolutions but late-night television as well. Distaste for the bureaucratic state got to the point where people could not imagine that anything they liked and valued was actually done by the government. President Bill Clinton used to tell of meeting an old woman who pressed his hands in hers and pleaded with him, "Please, please, Mr. President, don't let the government ruin my Medicare."

Dissatisfaction with government manifested itself in more concrete ways in a tax revolt that spread across the United States beginning in 1978 with passage of Proposition 13 in California. The proposition put a ceiling on property taxes that was quickly copied elsewhere in the country. Even liberal politicians became reluctant to raise taxes, and conservative politicians came to use lower taxes as a mantra for all the ills of the country.

In the meantime, however, no one seriously suggested that government actually should do less. Local governments were expected to fix potholes and run school systems; state governments were expected to manage public health systems and fund universities. When the conservative, antigovernment movement in the United States finally bore fruit in 1994 with the Republican takeover of the US House of Representatives, for the first time in more than forty years, conservative political elites hoped for great changes that liberal political elites feared. But even then, with the wind at their backs and decades of pent-up antigovernment sentiment, the conservative revolution failed to deliver any substantive reduction in government. So a conservative, antitax, antigovernment majority has now controlled Congress for most of the past decade and, with the exception of changes related to 9/11, such as the creation of the Department of Homeland Security, the government does not look appreciably different now than it did then.

So how can we explain the growth in citizen distrust of government that so permeated politics in the last decades of the twentieth century? One explanation is that as the century wore on citizens began to perceive a disconnect between the aspirations of policymakers and the realities of policy implementation. As distrust grew, political scientists turned their attention to problems in policy implementation—much of which was fueled by unhappiness with Great Society programs, mostly from the 1960s. In 1973 Jeffrey Pressman and Aaron Wildavsky took on the problem in a book whose subtitle says it all: *Implementation: How Great Expectations in Washington are Dashed in Oakland*.[6]

Focusing empirically on policy implementation across a variety of government programs forced scholars to confront some of their most firmly held beliefs. In looking at implementation they found that it was complex enough to sometimes alter original policy decisions, thus blurring traditional distinctions between policy and implementation. Daniel A. Mazmanian and Paul A. Sabatier worried that viewing policymaking and implementation as a "seamless web" would "obscure" one of the "principal normative and empirical concerns of scholars interested in public policy, namely the division of authority between elected public officials (primarily legislators) on the one hand, and appointed and career administrative officials on the other."[7]

Yet another set of scholars began to focus on the multitude of actors involved in the operation of government. This "bottom-up" approach was brought home to the scholarly community in a 1983 book by Michael Lipsky. Lipsky introduced the concept of the street-level bureaucrat into the lexicon and with it the notion that what happened at the street level in a bureaucracy could be fundamentally disconnected from what the policymakers thought would happen.[8]

By the 1990s, continuing dissatisfaction with policy implementation had contributed to the growth of a powerful criticism of bureaucracy. The traditional literature, which focused either on top-down or bottom-up analysis gave way to a new set of concerns focused on performance.[9] In *Breaking through Bureaucracy*, published in 1992, Michael Barzelay showed how the modern bureaucratic paradigm had managed to turn bureaucracies into organizations that were often dysfunctional even when—or especially when—operating according to the rules.[10] By the end of the twentieth century such authors as Derek Bok, Christopher Pollitt and Geert Bouckaert, Neal Ryan, Cheryl Barnes and Derek Gill, and Harvey Sims, representing a cross-section of the Anglo-American world, were all arguing what the politicians had intuited all along: citizen mistrust of government had its roots in failing government performance.[11] Organization performance began to replace the worries of an earlier generation about the relationship between policymakers and their legal and/or legislative mandates.

In the meantime, in the face of citizen distrust and doubts about policy implementation, elected politicians and civil servants still had to govern. Late-twentieth-century political culture presented those who governed with an interesting dilemma—How do you govern in an era when the public yells "Do something!" at regular intervals, about problems ranging from bad meat in hamburgers to terrorists in the subways, and yet they further yell, "And don't let the government do it!"

This barrage of contradictory messages begat one of the most creative periods in the history of governance. The movement to "reinvent government," as it was dubbed in the United States, or the "new public management," as it was called in the other Anglo-American countries at the forefront of this movement, began in Great Britain in 1982, in New Zealand in 1984, in US statehouses in the 1980s, and in the US federal government in 1993. In Great Britain the first part of the Thatcher revolution involved the privatization of state-owned industries (in fact, through much of the 1980s, government reform consisted of just this). As Great Britain began undoing its quasi-socialist past other countries watched and followed suit. Although the US president at the time, Ronald Reagan, was a fellow conservative and great friend of Margaret Thatcher, the US government did not change very much during this period. Industries being nationalized in other parts of the world had never been nationalized in the first place in the United States.

Having weathered the brutal politics of privatization, the Thatcher government turned next to operations of the core government. There, under Minister Michael Heseltine, Thatcher established The Efficiency Unit, a revolutionary office that began the process of bringing private-market accountability for results to the civil service. The eventual report of this unit

> argued that to solve the management problem, the government would have to separate service-delivery and compliance functions from the policy-focused departments that housed them—to separate steering from rowing. Second, it would have to give service-delivery and compliance agencies much more flexibility and autonomy. And third, it would have to hold those agencies for results, through performance contracts.[12]

As Britain was remaking its large government bureaucracies into more entrepreneurial organizations, New Zealand was undergoing an even more dramatic revolution. In the mid-1980s New Zealand was facing an economic and political meltdown of striking proportions. As the new Labour government took over in 1987, it published a postelection briefing paper described as the "manifesto" of the new public management.[13] The New Zealand experience was unique for its boldness, continuity, and intellectual coherence. It is no wonder that for many of the years at the end of the twentieth century, government reform seemed to have outstripped lamb as the most popular New Zealand export.

Like the Thatcher reforms, the New Zealand reforms injected the language of competition, incentives, and performance into public administration. These reforms were remarkable in absolute terms, and against the quasi-socialist dogmas of previous governments they were extraordinary. They called for getting the government out of those activities that could be more effectively carried out by nongovernment bodies. They called for a clear separation of the responsibilities of ministers and department heads, thus giving the traditional civil service both more autonomy and more responsibility for results than ever before. And, perhaps the most revolutionary aspect of all was the directive that *everything* publicly funded—even policy advice—was to be made "contestable and subject to competitive tendering."[14] Cabinet ministers "purchased" government outputs from what used to be the bureaucracy, and the bureaucracy was forced to "compete" with other public- or private-sector organizations to do the work of the government.[15] New Zealand broke the public monopoly of government on governance. While officials in the United States were still asking what core government functions were, New Zealand had decided the answer was, in essence, nothing.

Reinvented government started at the national level in Britain and New Zealand, but in the United States this revolution in government management started at the state and local level. Unlike the federal government, statehouses cannot print their own money. Forced to live within their means and buffeted by tax revolts on one side and continued demands for services on the other, mayors and governors in the 1970s and 1980s had no choice but to try to do more with less, even if it meant stepping on some toes. When Ed Rendell took over as mayor of the troubled city of Philadelphia in the late 1980s he quickly recognized that he could raise taxes (and push even more of the tax base to the suburbs) or he could cut services (and achieve exactly the same result).[16] As a Democratic mayor he had no choice but to take on the status quo—including the powerful public-sector unions—and reinvent government. The Republican mayor of Indianapolis, Steve Goldsmith, got national attention when he put twenty-seven city services out for private-sector bids. In Minnesota, the governor set about dismantling the government's central-control mechanisms and reconstructing them in ways that would add to, not detract from, agency missions.[17] (This insight, that central-control mechanisms were becoming inimical to government performance, was the centerpiece of Michael Barzelay's book.)

For US state and local officials, and for British and New Zealand national officials in the 1980s, reinvented government was the only way out of an impossible governance situation. What began as an adaptation to budget crises evolved, however, into a more or less coherent philosophy. This movement hit the US federal government in 1993, when Vice President Al Gore, at the request of President Clinton, inaugurated the National Performance Review (NPR).[18]

For Clinton and Gore, reinventing government solved the very tricky political problem of how a Democrat talks about government in a political culture that is vehemently antigovernment, By adapting the mantra of reform in the 1992 presidential campaign, Bill Clinton managed to soften the suspicion the electorate held about Democrats when it came to government. That and his other "new Democrat" credentials, along with a not insignificant boost from Ross Perot, managed to put him in the White House where he quickly put his vice president in charge of the effort to reinvent government.

The initial report of the National Performance Review, as the effort was known, was drafted by David Osborne and a team of reform-minded civil servants. It echoed and crystallized many of the criticisms that had been made of bureaucratic government. For instance, there was this one: "Is government inherently incompetent? Absolutely not. Are federal agencies filled with incompetent people? No. The problem is much deeper: Washington is filled with organizations designed for an environment that no longer exists—bureaucracies so big and wasteful they can no longer serve the American people."[19]

The Information Age

By the beginning of the twenty-first century the Anglo-American experiments in postbureaucratic government were well documented and the topic of several international conferences.[20] David Osborne's 1988 book, *Laboratories of Democracy,* chronicled the innovative efforts of US governors as they coped with governing in an era when no one liked government.[21] His next book, *Reinventing Government: How the Entrepreneurial Spirit is Transforming the Public Sector,* written with Ted Gaebler in 1993, coined the phrase that came to represent efforts at government reform in the United States and achieved the distinction of being a book about government that both appeared on the best seller list and that went on to inspire the reform efforts of the Clinton-Gore administration.[22]

Others were busy chronicling this revolution in policy implementation as well. In 1996, B. Guy Peters wrote a book called *The Future of Governing,* which discussed four emerging models of government: market, participative, flexible, and deregulated, government, which all sought to solve one or more problems of the traditional bureaucratic state.[23] By 2002, Lester M. Salamon was able to put together his mammoth work, *The Tools of Government,* that documented all the alternative policy implementation modes that had come to constitute a revolution "in the 'technology' of public action over the last fifty years."[24]

That government policy should be implemented through "nonbureaucratic" means is now taken for granted in many of the world's most advanced democracies. In Great Britain, Tony Blair's Labour Party ("New Labour") kept most of the important Thatcher innovations and expanded upon them by paying more attention to electronic government, by pushing the government toward "joined-up" government (an effort to get government agencies to work across boundaries), and by introducing competition and contestability into the provision of public services.[25] To the intense discomfort of the privileged British civil service, the Blair government centralized policymaking in Number Ten Downing Street (in what was deemed a "presidential system") in order to more closely control policy. This was a necessary innovation because among the policies he wanted to drive were change in the civil service itself.[26]

In the United States, the Bush administration kept many if not most of the Clinton-Gore reforms and added to them its own "President's Management Agenda." This included a renewed emphasis on electronic government, a human capital agenda that emphasized, among other things, performance and goal setting, a mandate on competitive sourcing or having agencies ask carefully whether a function should be done in house or contracted out, and an award-winning addition to the Office of Management and Budget (OMB) performance process, the Performance Assessment Rating Tool, which assigns scores to government programs to rate their effectiveness.[27] In New Zealand, the dramatic reforms of the 1980s persisted through a series of governments under both political parties although the reforms have now been modified by the addition of "circuit breaker teams, a new emphasis on partnerships, managing for outcomes...[which are] an understandable response to the excesses of earlier reforms."[28]

Dramatic changes in governance are most clearly associated with the Anglo-American countries but they are common throughout Western Europe. France amended its constitution in 2001 to allow for the modernization of public management—its first constitutional amendment since 1959. Italy began a decade of reform in the early 1990s under the leadership of Franco Bassanini, minister of public administration reform, and is now investing heavily in digital government. The European Organisation for Economic Co-operation and Development (OECD) has catalogued the full range of public-administration reforms throughout the world's most developed countries.

The result is that almost all the world's most advanced democracies now implement policy in a wide variety of ways. To be sure, there are still traditional bureaucracies, but they exist alongside new and reformed bureaucratic structures, an array of public-private partnerships—such as contracting out, networked government, or coproduced government, to name a few—and the use of state power to create incentives for certain behaviors where there were none before. In other words, twenty-first-century government is a messy blend of old-fashioned bureaucracy, partly and fully privatized government, and markets.

It is not surprising that there is no consensus and that there is some controversy over this hodgepodge of means of government. Both ends of the political spectrum see what they want to see. The right wing believes that most government functions could be done better by the private sector; the left wing suspects that any addition of the private sector to the public sphere unfairly enriches the former and undermines the common good.

As in most complex problems both are right and both are wrong. The choice of means and whether or not it contributes to the public good depends on a set of factors having to do with the characteristics of the policy objective at hand and the management of public-sector implementation. Now that we have a decade or more of experience with these new governmental forms, a nonideological look requires us to admit that there have been some stunning successes and some stunning failures. It is time to take a clear-headed look at modern methods of policy implementation and try to match policy problems to implementation methods to understand how best to serve the public interest.

Chapter 2 summarizes these new modes of implementation, placing them in three general categories: reinvented public-sector organizations, government by network, and government by market. And this chapter shows how the categories can be matched to their optimal implementation mode by breaking policy problems down by type. It concludes with a matrix for matching means to ends.

Of course, efficacy and efficiency are not the only measures of effective public policy, which is why Chapter 3 explores the issues of democratic accountability and the trade-offs in accountability that accompany each new mode of policy implementation. Chapter 4 looks at the failure of the bureaucratic instinct in two very different policy areas that will be considered throughout this book, welfare dependence and homeland security, and concludes with a matrix for the evaluation of each policy problem.

Beginning in the second half of the book, chapters describe each implementation mode in more depth and then apply it to our two policy examples. For instance, Chapter 5 describes the characteristics of reinvented public-sector organizations and looks at those aspects of welfare dependence and homeland security that are best dealt with through such organizations. Chapter 6 describes the characteristics of government by network and goes on to describe how government by network applies to parts of the welfare dependence and homeland security problems. Chapter 7 looks at the characteristics of government by market and contains examples of how government by market is or could be applied to the policy problems of welfare dependence and homeland security.

In Chapter 8, the book concludes with some thoughts on how the existence of these new policy implementation tools change not only the leadership skills required of public-sector leaders in the future but the oversight roles of legislative bodies.

Notes

1. Donald Inglehart, "Postmodernization Erodes Respect for Authority but Increases Support for Democracy," *Critical Citizens: Global Support for Democratic Governance,* ed., Pippa Norris (Oxford: Oxford University Press, 1999).

2. Joseph Nye Jr. et al., ed., *Why People Don't Trust Government* (Cambridge: Harvard University Press, 1997).

3. Ibid. For the absence of a clear relationship between economic performance and declining trust, see chapter 4, "Is It Really the Economy, Stupid?" For a discussion of government accomplishment in the face of declining trust, see chapter 2, "Measuring the Performance of Government."

4. Gary Orren,"Fall from Grace: The Public's Loss of Faith in Government" in ibid., 84.

5. For a wonderful history of these leaders, see Donald Savoie, *Thatcher, Reagan and Mulroney* (Pittsburgh: University of Pittsburgh Press, 1994), 6.

6. Jeffrey L. Pressman and Aaron Wildavsky, *Implementation: How Great Expectations in Washington Are Dashed in Oakland* (Berkeley: University of California Press, 1973).

7. Daniel A. Mazmanian and Paul A. Sabatier, *Implementation and Public Policy* (Glenview, IL: Scott, Foresman and Company, 1983), 8.

8. Michael Lipsky, *Street Level Bureaucracy* (New York: Russell Sage Foundation, 1983).

9. See Paul A. Sabatier, "Top-Down and Botton-Up Approaches to Implementation Research: A Critical Analysis and Suggested Synthesis," *Journal of Public Policy* 6, 1 (1986): 21–48.

10. Michael Barzelay, *Breaking Through Bureaucracy,* (Berkeley: University of California Press, 1992).

11. Derek Bok, *The Trouble with Government,* (Cambridge, MA: Harvard University Press, 2001); Neal Ryan, "Public Confidence in the Public Sector" (Discussion paper, Office of the Auditor General of Western Australia, 2001); Cheryl Barnes and Derek Gill, "Declining Government Performance? Why Citizens Don't Trust Government" (Working paper 9, New Zealand State Services Commission, 2000); Christopher Pollitt and Geert Bouckaert, *Public Management Reform: A Contemporary Analysis* (New York: Oxford University Press, 2000); Harvey Sims, "Public Confidence in Government and Government Service Delivery" (Ottawa: Canadian Center for Management Development, 2001).

12. David Osborne and Peter Plastrick, *Banishing Bureaucracy: The Five Strategies for Reinventing Government* (Reading, MA: Addison-Wesley, 1997), 25.

13. Johnathan Boston et al., *Public Management, the New Zealand Model* (Auckland: Oxford University Press, 1996).

14. Ibid., 5.

15. See Tim Irwin, "An Analysis of New Zealand's New System of Public Sector Management," in *Public Management in Government: Contemporary Illustrations,* OECD Occasional Papers 9, Paris, 1996.

16. Conversation between Mayor Rendell and the author.

17. Barzelay, *Breaking Through Bureaucracy*.

18. The author was senior policy adviser to Vice President Gore and had primary responsibility for creation and management of the NPR.

19. Vice President Al Gore, *Creating a Government That Works Better and Costs Less* (Report of the National Performance Review) (Washington, DC: Government Printing Office, September 10, 1993), 3.

20. The first international conference on reinventing government was sponsored by the Kennedy School of Government at Harvard and the US government. Since then international conferences focusing on government reforms have been held in Brazil, Italy, Morocco, Mexico, and Korea, and the UN Office of Public Administration has played an important role in these conferences.

21. David Osborne, *Laboratories of Democracy* (Boston: Harvard Business School Press, 1988).

22. David Osborne and Ted Gaebler, *Reinventing Government: How the Entrepreneurial Spirit Is Transforming the Public Sector* (New York: Plume, 1993).

23. B. Guy Peters, *The Future of Governing: Four Emerging Models* (Lawrence: University Press of Kansas, 1993).

24. Lester Salamon, ed., "The New Governance and the Tools of Public Action: An Introduction," *The Tools of Government: A Guide to the New Governance* (New York: Oxford University Press, 2002).

25. Vernon Bognador, *Joined Up Government* (New York: Oxford University Press, 2005).

26. See Peter Hennessy, *The Prime Minister: The Office and its Holders Since 1945*," (New York: Palgrave/St. Martin's, 2001), 476–493. See also *The UK Government's Approach to Public Service Reform*, June 2006 (London: The Prime Minister's Strategy Unit).

27. This program won the Innovations in Government Award in 2005, which is sponsored by the Kennedy School of Government at Harvard University. See www.innovations.edu.

28. E-mail from Tim Tenbensel, Department of Political Studies, University of Auckland, March 22, 2004.

2

Matching Means to Ends

IN DEMOCRATIC SOCIETIES the policymaking process goes through two major stages: deciding what to do and how to do it. The first step can take years. It took decades for a comprehensive health care program for the elderly to make it from the platform of the Democratic Party into law. It took about a decade for the country to reform a welfare system that was not working. We are still arguing about the future of the social security system, the use of coal for energy, whether or not we buy too much Middle East oil, and many other topics. In the past, however, once the first step was settled and the political process yielded a consensus on *what* to do, policymakers did not have too many arguments over *how* to do it. They created a bureaucracy or gave the task to an already existing one.

Given the degree of innovation in government in the past two decades, policymakers in the twenty-first century will not have to settle for bureaucracy; once they have decided what to do, they will be able to choose *how* to do it. This process will be no more free of political discord than the decision about what to do, for there will be winners and losers, depending on the implementation method chosen. But these new modes of policy implementation bring a new and important dimension to the business of government by allowing us to separate, more than ever before, the question of ends from the question of means.

Each new mode of government implementation that has appeared in the past two decades has been an attempt to correct the problems and dilemmas associated with traditional bureaucracy: poor performance, deficit of flexibility, and paucity of innovation. Often, however, these new forms of implementation have been applied to policy problems without fully thinking through the forms' strengths and weaknesses and whether or not they are suited to the policy problem at hand.

It is well established that certain kinds of policy goals require certain kinds of implementation approaches. Many years ago Pressman and

15

Wildavsky wrote, "The separation of policy design from implementation is fatal. It is no better than mindless implementation without a sense of direction."[1] In the years since, many scholars have studied implementation. In his survey of the implementation literature Richard Matland concludes that research on the topic divides into two camps, those who look at implementation from the top down and those who look at implementation from the bottom up. The former works better with unambiguous policy goals, while the latter works better with the ambiguous policy goals.[2]

Considering modern implementation methods alongside an analysis of policy goals will broaden the possibilities resulting from public action. All too often, the government's intent or desire to solve a problem is simply not matched by its ability. The usual way to think of this is as a financial problem (i.e., government has trouble solving public problems because it does not have enough money). But financial problems will always be with us, and modern government is filled with examples where money does not seem to be the answer.

This book will argue that government in the twenty-first century faces a technological choice and opportunity. We have expanded the technology of government beyond bureaucracy, but to maximize the potential of the twenty-first-century state for achieving the public goals we need to make the appropriate match between policy and implementation. In so doing we ought to be able to increase the efficacy of government and create one more attuned to the complexity and need for flexibility that is characteristic of public policy problems of the twenty-first century.

As we saw in Chapter 1, many writers have described the implementation tools in use in modern governments. For the purposes of this book I summarize these new tools in three categories: reinvented government, government by network, and government by market. I will expand on these definitions in subsequent chapters, but to lay out the model for analysis that characterize this book I summarize them as follows.

Reinvented Government

I use "reinvented government" to refer to public-sector organizations that operate without the trappings of traditional bureaucracy. In these organizations, performance measures[3] act as market proxies, allowing government to compete against measures set for itself and against other, similarly situated governments (or in some cases against similar private-sector institutions). In these organizations the dominance of such central-control mechanisms as budget rules, personnel rules, and procurement rules is traded for enhanced flexibilities. In these organizations customer service is used to model organizational behavior vis-à-vis the citizen even though it is clear that the citizen is not exactly a "customer." And in these organizations information technology is used to increase productivity. In other words, reinvented government is government that is run as much like a private-sector business as is possible.

Government by Network

In government by network, the bureaucracy is replaced by a wide variety of other kinds of institutions. The government stops trying to do everything itself and funds other organizations that do the actual work the government wants done. The variety of organizations that can constitute government by network is immense. Churches, university and private research laboratories, nonprofit and for-profit organizations are all called upon to perform the work of the government. When a state opts to create a network it is because its leaders want things to happen that would not occur to the same extent without the resources and direction of the state. Networks can be composed of other government organizations, such as state and local governments, or they can be made up of non-governmental organizations (NGOs). The defining characteristic is that they are all contracted by a state entity using state money for something that the private market would not produce, to the extent required, on its own.

Government by Market

Reinvented government and government by network are both different from bureaucratic government but they both involve a significant amount of government as we know it. In reinvented government organizations the public's work is done by people who work for the government. In government by network, much of the public's work is paid for by the government even though it is not performed by government employees and not constrained by all a government's protocols and central-control mechanisms. In the third category of implementation, government by market, the work of government involves few, if any, public employees and little or no public money. The government uses state power to create a market that fulfills a public purpose, and by definition that kind of market would not exist in the private sector. Often this involves taking into account what economists call "externalities." If reinvented government is government dressed up to look like the private sector and government by network is government that hides behind much more popular organizations, government by market is so well disguised that most people are not even aware that it is government in its operation. Because of this it is the model furthest from traditional bureaucratic government.

Matching Policies to Implementation

Creating a matrix for the application of implementation to policy takes two basic steps: breaking down a policy problem into its various components and matching each subset of a policy problem to the most appropriate implementation mode.

For instance, some components of a policy problem have unambiguous goals and are therefore subject to routinization. Others require a high level of security. When the two occur together, the objective can be best met by reinvented public-sector organizations. Issuing passports, drivers' licenses, or other forms of legal identification and determining eligibility for government benefits are two examples of policy that can be routinized. In theory these functions could be performed by a network of organizations under contract to the state, but given how important legal documents are to identity and security, the problems associated with allowing any other but the public sector a role in this process are enormous. And, given how important it is for the state to control the amount of benefits it pays out and the fairness with which the benefits are distributed, it makes sense that the public sector should control this process as well. Thus the best implementation tool is probably reinvented government.

But just because a function is best implemented within the public sector does not mean that it cannot incorporate modern business practices—especially customer service—in its routines. It used to be that if you had to go abroad at the last minute and your passport had expired, you were required to go through a rather elaborate explanation and show the urgency of your trip to get an expedited passport. These days you simply show your travel dates, pay more money, and the consular service will renew your passport quickly. User fees, Internet information and transactions, Saturday and evening business hours all help make the reinvented public-sector organization more efficient and responsive to their citizens.

Benefits are another area where public-sector organizations should retain control. Access to government benefits is intended to be universal under the law; in other words, all citizens should be able to get benefits if they qualify. And governments have an interest in trying to control the costs of benefit programs by reducing fraud. A network system of determining Social Security or pension or welfare eligibility would be hard to police and probably open to more fraud than exists today. But even though the state has an overwhelming interest in maintaining control over the establishment of government benefits, it can use modern technology and customer service techniques to ease the establishment of those benefits to citizens and to reduce its own costs.

Other public-policy problems require flexibility and innovation. We do not want flexibility in determining whether poverty-stricken mothers are entitled to welfare benefits, but we do know from experience that what works to get one welfare mother into a job may require a substantial amount of flexibility and innovation. Getting welfare mothers to work is one of many government problems to which there is no one answer. Government by network allows the government to provide a range of options to certain policy problems. For this reason many social services in the United States have traditionally been made available through some form of network where the providers of the services take different and often innovative approaches to the problems. People problems, or "sticky" problems as they are referred to in political science, do not lend themselves to standard routines. The bureaucratic model has never worked well in this kind of policy area.

Similarly, government has played an enormously important role in society by sponsoring pure research. Although government laboratories have been prolific and important, the US government's implementation choice for basic research has never been bureaucracy, but always been some form of network. When it comes to research, government by network has two major attractions. Unlike bureaucratic government it has the potential to be flexible and to innovate, characteristics in short supply in traditional bureaucracies. Second, government by network is often used when the government values innovation so much that it is willing to give up some degree of control.

The longest-standing example of networked government is the famous "military-industrial complex." The offensive and defensive capacity of the US military goes well beyond its actual operational assets because of its ability to expand and innovate rapidly. Faced with the need for massive mobilization at the beginning of World War II, President Roosevelt did not nationalize the industrial might of the nation, but used instead the government's financial and other powers to create a network of participants in the war effort. As we discovered during World War II, US military might rested as much on the ability to produce weaponry in the private sector for itself and all its allies as it did on the ability of its soldiers, seamen, and airmen to fight.

During the succeeding Cold War the model remained the same. Seeking ever-better weapons against the Soviet Union, the United States engaged countless corporations, universities, and private laboratories, along with its own internal research laboratories, in the development of sophisticated weaponry. In the kind of controlled experiment that rarely happens in the real world, the totalitarian Soviet Union kept its weapons research within its all-encompassing bureaucracy. By 1989 the experiment was over. When the Soviet empire fell, we learned, among other things, that its technological and military capacity had fallen well behind that of the United States. Government by network had won; bureaucratic government had lost. [4]

Finally, government by market is the best, and sometimes only, realistic implementation option when a policy consensus is reached that requires many hundreds of businesses or many thousands of people to change their behaviors. Government by market is especially important in an era where citizens place a high value on personal choice and in an era in which scientific and technological changes happen so quickly that the law cannot keep up.

For instance, one of the lessons of the 1960s and 1970s was that government job creation for the poor did not work very well. In fact, as a policy option it has been largely abandoned in favor of a tax subsidy (i.e., the earned income tax credit) for people with low-income jobs in the private sector. Instead of trying to create jobs for the poor through the government, a more successful antipoverty strategy has been to subsidize, through the tax system, the low-paying jobs that poor people most often find for themselves.

In the field of environmental regulation policymakers have increasingly turned to setting performance goals and away from dictating technologies for the achievement of the goals. Individual chemical factories and plants can be far more creative than legislators and rule writers when it comes to figuring out ways to reduce pollution. One of these programs, the Environmental Protection Agency's 33/50 program, "achieved its goal of 50 percent reduction in releases and transfers of seventeen targeted chemicals one year ahead of schedule."[5]

In a free society, any public policy whose goal is to change the behaviors of millions of people must use government by market. The degree of coercion required to police beverage bottle disposal or gasoline consumption is simply unthinkable outside of an extreme emergency or a police state. Thus when states decide to increase recycling, they do not create bureaucracies dedicated to that purpose, they create a market in bottles. If we as a society ever come to a consensus on using smaller amounts of fossil fuels, we will do it through some sort of government by market that allows hundreds of millions of people to find their own adaptations to achieve the overall goal.

Table 2.1 begins to categorize types of policy problems by their optimal mode of implementation and gives some examples. The first box on the chart contains functions like issuing passports or drivers' licenses. These are easily routinized and for security reasons are best kept within the exclusive control of the public sector. It is hard to find the most hard-core libertarian advocating a private-sector market in either one. On the other hand, fishing and hunting licenses are not nearly as important to the state as are passports. Although such licenses are required by states, purchasing them at bait shops or at campgrounds is regularly allowed. Thus the government lets a network do much of the actual work of processing and selling the license. The difference is that unlike with a passport, most people do not think a fishing license requires a high degree of security.

Table 2.1   Types of Public Policy Problems and Their Optimal Implementation Mode (Examples)

	Reinvented Public-Sector Organizations	Government by Network	Government by Market
The public policy in question can be routinized and/or requires a high level of security.	Issuing passports; issuing drivers' licenses; determining eligibility for benefits; airport security.	Issuing fishing or hunting licenses.	
The public policy in question requires flexibility and innovation.		Getting welfare mothers to work; treating the mentally ill; collecting intelligence on terrorism; research and development.	Getting factories to come up with ways of reducing environmentally harmful emissions.
The public policy in question requires that millions of people behave in a certain way or change their behavior.			Getting people to return empty bottles; creating a market for tradable permits; getting people to stop driving gas-guzzling cars; issuing vouchers to parents to use day care; subsidizing low-income work.

Airport security, however, is a different matter. Before September 11, 2001 (9/11), airport security was a classic example of government by network. The Federal Aviation Administration (FAA) mandated that the airlines pay for screening procedures at each airport. It also set standards and rules to be followed by the companies, the cost being borne by the airlines that, up until 9/11, had had years without a terrorist incident or hijacking in the United States. Since security was not seen as a problem and because it was not tied to the airlines' bottom line, the money spent on security was minimal—and it showed. Following 9/11, Congress quickly passed a law creating the Transportation Security Administration (TSA), placing airport security firmly under the control of the federal government.

But just because airline security is in the public sector does not mean that it cannot take ideas from the private sector to improve its operations. Just as the passport office finally realized that people would pay the cost of expedited passport renewals, the TSA is slowly waking up to the fact that frequent travelers will pay the cost and undergo the scrutiny necessary to move through airports more quickly. In the works are plans that allow travelers to submit themselves to extra scrutiny. This kind of program is typical of reinvented government. It uses concepts from the private sector to try to reduce the workload—in this instance, lines at airports. But the program does not coerce anyone into such scrutiny, thus preserving privacy, and the government retains control over who gets the special quick passes, thus preserving security.

Government by network works best on policy problems that require flexibility, personalization, and innovation, which is why it has become and will continue to be the preferred mode of action for the delivery of social services in the United States. As we will see, it was no accident that the old welfare system turned into one obsessed with the accuracy of its eligibility determinations. Not only was that the federal mandate that came down to states, but eligibility was a task, bound by rules and uniformity that bureaucracy was good at enforcing. Similarly, the post–World War II intelligence community was a bureaucracy adept at monitoring another bureaucracy—that of the Soviet Union. It has, however, proved ill equipped in monitoring loose networks of terrorists.

Scientific research cannot, by its very nature, be routinized; any attempts to define scientific inquiry a priori are doomed to failure. One of the concerns expressed frequently in the debate over stem cell research is that by limiting the research to certain lines, the Bush administration is dooming the nation to second place in the race to cure various diseases.

Government by market works best on those policy problems that require hundreds, thousands, or millions of individuals or organizations to achieve a public-policy end. Those old enough to remember Lady Bird Johnson (wife of President Lyndon Johnson) are old enough to remember that she waged a battle to clean up the country's highways, which in the 1960s were beginning to be buried by beer cans and soft-drink bottles. By the 1970s these containers posed serious problems for public cleanliness and proper disposal. The solution to the problem came from government. In 1971 Oregon passed the nation's first "bottle bill." But instead of creating a bureau of clean highways and hiring workers to pick up bottles, government did something unusual: it created a market. By passing laws that required deposits on beverage bottles and cans, government created an economic incentive to keep people from throwing bottles out of their cars. And for the hard-core litterbugs who persisted in such behavior, the laws created an economic incentive for other people to pick them up.[6]

Similarly, in the 1991 Clean Air Bill, Congress decided to put a price on sulfur dioxide (SO_2) emissions from industrial plants. (Sulfur dioxide is the primary cause of acid rain.) The government determined how much SO_2 the environment could handle and then developed a trading system, which allowed clean plants to "sell" permits and dirty plants to "buy" them. Most analysts feel this system has worked: in the past thirty years, emissions trading (and other improvements) have caused nearly a 50 percent drop in the amount of SO_2 in the air.[7] The "price" was high enough to encourage plants to get new equipment for cleaner air but low enough for them to determine their own timetable.

Government by market has also been used to augment the wages of low-income workers and to provide choice in day care to working parents. If the US government ever gets serious about reducing its dependence on fossil fuels, most of the options on the table will almost certainly be government by market because a free society cannot expect to alter the behavior of millions of citizens in any other way.

Conclusion

As Table 2.1 illustrates, policy problems can be broken down by type and matched to their optimal implementation mode. Doing this reduces the ideological component of the decision considerably. It is hard to imagine the most conservative libertarian advocating that the marketplace ought to provide people with drivers' licenses, and it is hard to picture the most pro-government liberal arguing that bureaucrats ought to pick up bottles or control all cancer research. Thus we see the importance of matching ends to means, thereby decreasing political controversy and increasing the efficacy of the technology choice.

Notes

1. Jeffrey L. Pressm and and Aaron Wildavsky, *Implementation: How Great Expectations in Washington Are Dashed in Oakland* (Berkeley: University of California Press, 1973), p. xvii.

2. Richard E. Matland, "Synthesizing the Implementation Literature: The Ambiguity-Conflict Model of Policy Implementation," *Journal of Public Administration Research and Theory* 5, 2 (1995): 145–175.

3. In Great Britain and other countries, performance measures are often called targets.

4. See, for instance, the story of a Soviet scientist's experience with the system in Roald V. Sagdeev, *The Making of a Soviet Scientist: My Adventures in Nuclear Fusion and Space from Stalin to Star Wars* (New York: Wiley, 1995).

5. Daniel Esty, "Environmental Protection in the Information Age," *New York University Law Review* 79, 1 (April 2004): 146.

6. By 1987 ten states, accounting for 25 percent of the nation's population, had passed some form of bottle bill. See www.bottlebill.com.

7. Robert N. Stavins, "What Can We Learn from the Grand Policy Experiment? Lessons from SO_2 Allowance Trading," *Journal of Economic Perspectives* 12, 3 (Summer 1998): 69–88.

3

Democratic Accountability

IF INNOVATION, EFFICACY, and efficiency were the ultimate objectives of public-sector institutions, matching of policy to implementation would be relatively straightforward. But they are not. Democratic governments are ultimately judged on their accountability to citizens, as much if not more than on their efficiency. And thus the postbureaucratic state will be judged not only by its performance but by the degree to which it allows citizens to hold it accountable for its actions. As we will see, new forms of policy implementation change the definition of transparency, generate new accountability mechanisms and sometimes require a trade-off between innovation and accountability.

When it comes to accountability, modern though traditional bureaucratic government has one big advantage over its successors: every action is transparent because most actions are spelled out in copious detail, available (with some digging) to the public. In the Clinton-Gore administration the visuals for reinventing government initiatives reinforced the fact that an endless volume of paper was needed to spell out the rules and regulations of traditional bureaucratic government. At one event, the president and vice president appeared against a backdrop of forklifts filled with government documents (see Photo 3.1).

It is not unheard of for even medium-sized agencies in the federal government to have internal rules and regulations that take up hundreds of pages. For instance, as of 1994, the federal personnel manual ran to 10,000 pages before being retired by the Clinton-Gore administration. When I was in the federal government, I used to refer to these internal rules as the agency's "self-inflicted wounds" because they were usually additions to the legislated rules and regulations. In some cases they supplemented an already highly detailed legislative or judicial mandate (a problem that has been especially severe in the area of environmental policy implementation). The accountability culture of

(Official White House Photograph)

**Photo 3.1   President Bill Clinton and Vice President Al Gore
Promote Reinventing Government**

the traditional bureaucracy means that internal rules and regulations will persist long past the existence of any statute that inspired them in the first place.

A case in point was passage of a procurement reform bill in 1995 that gave agencies the authority to use credit cards and a simplified process for purchase of items under $2,500. Previous procurement rules had tended to treat the purchase of even a simple item such as a stapler as if it were an F-18 fighter plane. Consequently, once the paperwork and processing time was added on, ordinary items ended up costing the government much more than they cost in the private sector. And yet, as I discovered by visiting government offices, individual agencies retained internal rules that replicated or even expanded the defunct purchasing statute years after the passage of legislation simplifying the procedures for small purchases.

The persistence of these rule-based systems, with all their complexity and added costs, is explained by one simple fact. For the public servant and the politicians and public to whom they are ultimately accountable, the accountability systems of the traditional bureaucracies are straightforward, transparent, and clear. Every action—from the purchase of an office chair to the filling out of forms to establish benefits—has its rules. The performance of all actors in the system is judged not by performance but by their adherence to the rules.

In the late 1970s the US government added to every major federal office an inspector general (IG). For the most part, this position has been filled by a former law enforcement officer who reinforces the rule-based culture by monitoring internal infractions both large and small.[1] Although the rhetoric surrounding the creation of the IG offices is filled with references to "waste, fraud, and abuse," very few of the items included in the IG reports are serious enough to ever be referred to the Justice Department for criminal prosecution. Nonetheless, IG investigations terrify federal workers and political appointees. In the macro sense, the rule-based culture that the IGs supported added to waste instead of subtracting from it.

Rule-based accountability systems evolved in the United States and other countries as a way to combat governmental corruption. In addition to the IG offices, the rules are created and enforced by a variety of central-control offices. Budget offices were created to control spending and to make sure that it was for the "right" things, personnel offices were established to make sure that patronage was under control and that civil servants were appointed on merit, procurement offices were instituted to make sure that the government paid the lowest price and got the best deal it could.

Thus in the traditional bureaucracy accountability is defined as strict adherence to process. As for the trade-offs between innovation and accountability: the day-to-day incentive structure of the traditional bureaucracy favors adherence to process over innovation. Leaders in traditional bureaucracies become skilled at the management and production of uniform outcomes.

But the effort to control operations from the center inevitably came into conflict with performance. The very accountability mechanisms put in place to prevent fraud, waste, and abuse also prevented good government performance. As Bob Behn and others have pointed out, a system meant to deal with the problem of corruption ended up creating a government plagued by poor performance.[2] A book from 1996 has a provocative title that says it all: *The Pursuit of Absolute Integrity: How Corruption Control Makes Government Ineffective.*[3] The authors analyze the elaborate mechanisms put in place over decades to try to control corruption in the New York City Building Authority and in the New York City Police Department and their relative ineffectiveness fighting both corruption and crime.

The accountability mechanisms of the traditional bureaucracy tend to have a negative effect on the employees in those systems. In a brilliant article prepared for the Waldo Symposium at the Maxwell School of Citizenship and Public Affairs at Syracuse University, the scholar Laurence J. O'Toole says that "it can be argued, on the basis of both logic and evidence, that hierarchies encourage a dulling or depersonalizing of individuals' sense of responsibility for their own actions. There is a tendency for those populating large agencies, in other words, to develop a somewhat weakened or distanced sense of their causation and volition."[4]

This dulling results in the kinds of bureaucratic behavior that infuriate the public and depress organizational performance. Public servants in these systems are rewarded for overseeing a uniform process and for following rules. When faced with a crisis they tend to create more rules, because rules are the source of both personal and institutional security. The accountability and leadership problems in traditional bureaucracies are summed up in Table 3.1.

Reinvented Public-Sector Organizations

Reinvented government bureaucracies are still public entities, which are composed of public-sector employees and rely solely on public-sector funding and appropriations. However, reinvented government tends to be government shorn of its public-sector trappings, especially rigid rules regarding budgets, personnel, and procurement. The underlying assumption behind reinvented government, as practiced in anglophone countries that have undergone the most serious public-sector reform movements, is that with respect to management, there are few significant differences between the public and the private sectors. A second but equally important assumption behind these entrepreneurial governments is that the goals of public-sector organizations can be clearly articulated and measured.

Thus, in David Osborne's terminology, the "grand bargain" between bureaucrats seeking to remake their traditional bureaucracies and the

Table 3.1 Accountability and Leadership in Traditional Bureaucracy

Degree of Transparency	Accountability Mechanism	Accountability versus Innovation	Management Goals	Management Pitfalls
High	Rules and regulations	Low levels of innovation	Following rules, enforcing uniformity	Adherence to process, crowding out performance

elected officials who would hold them accountable on the public's behalf is one in which the strict, sometimes stultifying, rules of the organization are replaced by performance measures. There have been many experiments in implementing the grand bargain across the globe, but in three notable cases—New Zealand's experiment in contracting out government work, Britain's experiment in creating "next step" or "executive" agencies, and the US government's creation of the Government Performance and Results Act (GPRA)—the introduction of performance measures means that public servants must deal with accountability systems and incentives more like those faced by private-sector managers and less like those faced by traditional civil servants. Nonetheless, performance measures are usually imposed on top of the existing system of rules and regulations that public managers in the new reinvented organizations must still abide by. Thus the real impact of performance measures is to give public managers the incentives to change or to work around whatever rules that impede achievement of the measures set by the representatives of the elected government.

In the United States the movement toward explicit performance-based bureaucracy is not as prevalent as in countries like New Zealand and Great Britain. Passage of the GPRA tied the creation of performance goals to the congressional budgetary process in an effort to engage the legislative branch in the quest for performance. So far, however, there is little evidence that performance measurement is affecting Congress's appropriation behavior and, unlike in Great Britain, the performance goals of the US government rarely make the newspapers, let alone the front page. Appropriations seem to follow the policy preferences of the administration in power and the pressing needs for security in a more dangerous world.

But some of the difference may be due to the fact that the US government does very little that people care about in a direct sense. It does not run a health service or an education system as the British government does. It is mostly a great big automatic teller machine for states and localities. However, performance measures are much more powerful drivers of state and local government, for which measures of crime control, living conditions, cancer rates, or public education, are regularly featured as comparisons between cities and states.

Nevertheless performance measurement is still young and will eventually affect even the federal portion of this nation's government systems. Even though many of the performance measures set by the federal government in the initial stages were so low that they could easily be achieved, they still exist as a baseline for improvement by government agencies and their managers. The very existence of such government measures will prompt the possibility of productivity increases in the public sector—a key motivation in creating reinvented governments.

The emphasis on performance over process has already manifested itself in this country's civil servants' and political leaders' willingness to seek legislative exceptions to the old-fashioned control systems' impediments to agency performance. For instance, in 1996 when it became clear to the Clinton administration that the Republican-dominated Congress would not pass a civil service reform bill that the president could sign, Vice President Gore's NPR encouraged and aided agencies in their efforts to get out from under Title V—the Civil Service Bill. One by one, agencies went to their appropriators and their authorizers in Congress to fashion personnel systems better suited to their mission. As a result, by 2000 more than 50 percent of the civil service workforce was not covered by the civil service law but by "excepted" personnel systems.[5]

During the Bush administration the movement away from Title V intensified. The first test came because of the personnel system to be used by the newly created Department of Homeland Security. Democrats in Congress tried to retain the old system, especially the parts dealing with unions. The Bush administration used this issue to nationalize the 2002 midterm elections and was successful in creating the new department and a new personnel system. Subsequently the administration had the National Security Personnel System, covering 700,000 civilian Department of Defense (DOD) employees, written into law. This makes significant changes to the traditional civil service law, including replacing the general schedule for pay with a performance-based system.

In some cases, the move to reinvention was initiated by Congress in response to serious agency performance deficits. In the summer of 1995, the antiquated equipment at the FAA began to fail, creating a series of near-catastrophes at busy airports. As news stories correctly pointed out, the earlier long delays in replacing air traffic control equipment were part of the problem. That summer, terrified that they would be blamed for inaction in the face of numerous attempts to modernize the agency, members of Congress gave the FAA the freedom to design its own procurement rules and personnel rules. The frightening news stories prompted Congress to write what was essentially a blank check to the FAA. The newly created procurement system began showing results right away as procurement times for the purchase of new computers dropped from more than eighteen months to just under four.[6]

Similarly, in the summer of 1997 Congress held a series of sensational hearings featuring IRS agents harassing little old ladies and other sympathetic Americans. This resulted in passage of a major IRS reform bill that reinvented the agency along the lines of more flexible personnel and procurement.[7] And when the Bush administration set out to create a Department of Homeland Security it tried to incorporate many of the management flexibilities that are core concepts in reinvented public-sector organizations, including some modest authority to reprogram funds without prior congressional approval and substantial flexibilities in procurement and civil service laws.[8]

Reinvented government seeks to replace an accountability system built on rules and regulations with an accountability system based on performance. This creates an incentive for public managers to address organizational impediments to better performance—impediments often found in old-fashioned central-control mechanisms. As the emphasis moves to performance, public-sector managers will be expected to innovate. But innovation for such managers will often entail a deft political dance to remove the agency from statutory and regulatory restrictions put in place to ensure agency compliance with the law and to prevent corruption. Thus the managers in a reinvented-government agency will also have to be adroit politicians with close ties to elected officials who oversee their agencies.

Estelle B. Richman, currently secretary of public welfare for the state of Pennsylvania, is one such public leader. In the mid-1990s she created the Behavioral Health System for the city of Philadelphia, a model mental health program that had at its core the blending of three complex funding streams. The streams were Medicaid dollars taken from Medicaid managed care, state hospital dollars, and state mental health program dollars. Richman's leadership in pulling off this complex reorganization of bureaucratic funding streams won her one of the Innovations in American Government Awards in 1999.[9] To accomplish this reorganization of separate funding streams, Richman had to have a unique legal and practical understanding of government at the federal, state, and local levels; she was forceful and charismatic enough to do what few had thought possible.

But public managers who seek to break down old bureaucratic walls can be subjected to increased scrutiny. Bob Stone, one of the earliest and most famous new public managers and the project director for Al Gore's National Performance Review, exercised what he called "creative subversion" and in so doing was sometimes just one step ahead of trouble. In his book, *Confessions of a Civil Servant,* Stone refers to the time he reduced the DOD's incomprehensible tome of rules and regulations regarding the administration of military bases to a short book that could fit into a shirt pocket. For this, he was investigated by the DOD inspector general, who was sure there had to be something illegal if so many rules and regulations could be reduced to so few.[10] Stone knew the rules better than most and managed to be creative in a very long government career—attracting the attention of management guru Tom Peters, reinventing-government author David Osborne, and finally Al Gore.

The public managers of reinvented-government agencies will face continual suspicion from those organizations of the government that are accustomed to control. When the Clinton administration introduced the concept of Performance-Based Organizations (PBOs), the OMB attempted to create a "template" into which all PBOs would fit. This would undermine the very idea of the new organizations, which was to allow them to structure themselves according to their unique missions. And in spite of the fact that myriad exceptions and flexibilities to the federal government's personnel laws exist, the perception among the civil service that the Office of Personnel Management (OPM) will "regulate" the flexibilities in such a way as to make them impracticable or a cause for criticism keeps many public managers from sticking their necks out in the first place.

And finally, the public manager of a reinvented-government agency will find that sometimes his or her political leaders are not very interested in performance measures. Serious efforts to improve performance can often have unintended consequences and they can often upset entrenched constituencies. The first attempt to allow Americans to get their Social Security earnings records off the Internet blew up amid concerns over privacy. For instance, to the surprise of this author and others, divorced fathers, seeking to hide their true earnings from their former spouses, objected to their earnings being discovered by their former wives who would know all the information needed to get the records online. The program had to be pulled and retooled before it was acceptable to the public.

Another example of a reinvention effort that ended up causing a political problem comes from an attempt to reengineer the process by which a person could qualify for Social Security disability benefits. This proposal was opposed by SSA disability lawyers. Using the very powerful language of due process and rights for the disabled, this group managed to stop an effort designed to shorten the time it took for a disabled person's claims to be decided upon by the bureaucracy. However, these lawyers were paid according to the months of back benefits their clients were denied. For all their talk of due process, these lawyers had a financial interest in a drawn-out appeals process.

One more example is found in a major reinvention project launched in the mid-1990s that would have tied all the agencies in the US government dealing with imports and exports into one standardized electronic data system. The International Trade Data System (ITDS) would have increased efficiency and efficacy at the national borders. Progress on the ITDS was killed because the US Customs Service, the lead agency, felt threatened and because the importers and exporters realized that the new system might actually make their life more costly. (It was ultimately revived, but only in the aftermath of 9/11.)[11]

Finally there is this one that involves the Department of Homeland Security (DHS). When Clark Ervin Kent, the first inspector general of DHS, sought to focus on outcomes and not process, he found himself persona non grata with the political leadership and was forced out after only a year in office. Breaking the IG stereotype described earlier, Kent decided to focus on performance and tested the newly federalized airport security system. His teams of investigators were able to get weapons and explosives past screeners at fifteen US airports in 2003.[12] His aggressive focus on performance was not welcome at the White House and he ended up forced out of office.

Much of the system works against those who try to create reinvented public-sector organizations. Every complex bureaucracy that has ever existed has produced a community of "fixers," that is, people who make their living out of complexity. When the old Soviet Union system worked it worked because it tended to have a person in the middle of it who was a sort of "fixer" and who made the impossible demands of the centralized economy sort of work—for a price. In Washington DC and in every state capital in the United States there are hordes of lawyers and lobbyists who specialize in making the government work. These middlemen (and women) are often the biggest impediment to creating modern government organizations. They are well-to-do and powerful and they can dress up opposition to government reform in the most high-minded language. They are especially good at influencing (or frightening) the career-minded elected official for whom experimentation and innovation are likely to be fraught with problems. The ultimate audience for faster, leaner, reinvented public-sector organizations is the citizenry they serve, but along the way the major pitfall for the public-sector innovator is likely to be the elected officials caught in the middle.

Table 3.2 summarizes the issues in accountability and leadership for reinvented government.

Government by Network

Government by network comes with its own set of challenges for government managers. As in reinvented government, these challenges arise

Table 3.2   Accountability and Leadership in Reinvented Government

Degree of Transparency	Accountability Mechanism	Accountability versus Innovation	Management Goals	Management Pitfalls
Medium to high	Performance measures and goals replacing some rules and regulations	Medium levels of innovation	Managing the trade-offs between central control and performance; reducing traditional central control mechanisms; innovating within the law, using flexibilities in the law, changing law when necessary	Increased scrutiny of civil servants; tendency of elected officials to ignore performance in favor of traditional accountability measures

out of the accountability mechanisms, or the lack thereof, in government by network. Because government by network has often been a sort of "default" mode of government, very little attention has been paid to what makes for success with this kind of policy implementation. On one level, accountability in government by network can be defined as simply the sum total of the work of the individual entities in the network. This is difficult to ascertain and, perhaps, not very meaningful. Real accountability in government by network should seek to answer the question of whether this network is accomplishing the public purpose for which it was constructed.

That question goes far beyond "contract management," which has traditionally been defined as a low-level, bookkeeping kind of exercise. As part of the federal government's procurement reform effort that he led, Steven Kelman has argued that "the third element of strategic contracting management, the administration of contracts once they have been signed, has been the neglected stepchild of these efforts." He goes on to argue that opponents to contracting out government work, especially government employee unions, are quick to point out that no one is minding the store and that academics who warn of the creation of a "hollow state" are also sounding alarms.[13] Kelman argues forcefully for making contract management a key, rather than a peripheral, management expertise inside an agency and for recognizing "contract administration as in the first instance a management function."[14]

Kelman's call for upgrading contract management is critical for those agencies like the DOD that contract out a large part of their work. But it is even more critical when the government elects to do *all* its work through a network. Many grants to state and local governments are awarded on a formula basis. The federal government audits for financial compliance, and no one ever asks whether the money in the network is achieving the public purposes for which it was established. Unlike a reinvented public-sector organization that has one or two performance measures, government by network often exists without specific performance measures for the network as a whole. Thus transparency in government by network tends to be low, as does accountability.

Leadership of government by network requires the leader to understand causality and constantly evaluate the parts of the network to see how they are contributing to the goal of the network as a whole, and why. One of the chief advantages of government by network is that it allows for enormous innovation in a way even reinvented government could never do. Thus the public manager in government by network needs to be skilled in the evaluation of many different kinds of programs. Like the manager in reinvented government, the manager in government by network must be able to set performance goals for the overall endeavor, but unlike the latter manager must also be able to understand and analyze the contributions that parts of the network make to the overall endeavor. That means understanding the consequences of various strategies and why they work—a skill set very different from those described in the classic public administration literature. Robert Agranoff and Michael McGuire sum up the challenge as "the classical, mostly intra-organizational-inspired management perspective that has guided public administration for more than a century is simply inapplicable for multi-organizational, multi-governmental, and multi-sectoral forms of governing."[15]

The leader of a government network needs to combine the skills of a rigorous academic and an enterprising investigative journalist to find out what is working and why. Stephen Goldsmith and William D. Eggers point this out in their excellent attempt to give structure to government by network: "To achieve high performance in this environment, governments will need to develop core capabilities in a host of areas where today they have scant experience…conceptualizing the network, integrating it, and developing effective knowledge sharing practices across the network."[16]

But that alone will not ensure effective management of the network.

While the leaders of reinvented government need to muster the political support to overturn obsolete bureaucratic obstacles to more effective action, the leaders of government by network will need to muster the political support to throw out bad performers in the network and reward the good ones. The leaders of government by network need to be constantly learning from the players in the network and then adjusting the participants so that the overall performance of the network improves.

This kind of behavior, however, is a rarity for several reasons. First, the creators of networks often fashion the contracts that constitute the network along bureaucratic lines—consciously or unconsciously replicating the bureaucracy that the network was designed to replace. Peter Cove, CEO and founder of America Works, one of the oldest and most well-known welfare-to-work companies, describes the problem as follows:

> I have found that welfare bureaucracies value process rather than product; good intentions mean more than success in achieving the stated goal. So the people who design welfare-to-work programs and draft their contracts rely almost solely on measures of input—the number of social workers, caseworkers, and trainers in the program, or the number of people completing training or leaving with a résumé—to determine success.[17]

Second, all too often, relationships in many publicly funded networks are complicated by the protection of special interests and powerful politicians, and woe to the conscientious bureaucrat who tries to upset the relationship. Just as leaders in reinvented-government organizations find that their efforts are often opposed by those who make their living off government complexity, ineptitude, and inefficiency, leaders in government by network find that powerful interests protect individual players in the network. Therefore it does not pay to look too closely at the performance of individual parts of the network: that might lead to a need to replace an organization under the protection of a powerful godfather. None of this is very explicit. But, as Peter Cove points out, a contract system that focuses on process rather than product "permits implicit patronage arrangements to flourish."[18] In welfare-to-work networks the protected organizations are often grassroots entities with strong ties to local officials, especially at election time. In larger networks, such as the network of weapons manufacturers, the protected companies are often represented by powerful lobbyists or former high-ranking military personnel. The former officials use the financial power of the companies and the geographic dispersion of their subcontractors to build protection for parts of the network.

Finally, the soft underbelly of government by network presents the nearly 100 percent probability that, over time, some actor in some part of the network will make a mistake, steal money, or simply prove ineffective in a way that is big enough to attract public attention. In the broad sweep of history, the military-industrial complex may be remembered for winning the Cold War. Along the way, however, it has been plagued by recurring instances of widespread corruption, waste, fraud, and abuse and much maligned for its $500 coffee pots and hammers.

So far, the extensive contracting that has been part of the welfare-reform system seems to be working: there are many heroic stories of women emerging from dependence into employment and some early statistics to back up that success. But it is just a matter of time before one of the new (or one of the old) organizations in this business becomes involved in a scandal that reflects poorly upon the entire network.

So the real problem with government by network goes far beyond contract management alone. Managing government by network is a different and larger task than managing contracts even though the latter is a subset of the former. The real problem is the absence of an overall accountability mechanism, which results in little or no management of the network. Management in many networks is still defined by the terms of the old traditional bureaucracy, that is, audit the contracts periodically and make sure that no one is spending money on things it should not be spent on. While academics and think tanks occasionally get inspired to find out how a particular example of government by network is doing, the fact is that the government that is funding the bulk of the network often has little or no interest in finding out how the network is doing. Nor does it have any interest in systematizing learning from the wide variety of organizations and innovations operating in the network.

The ability to define performance and to constantly adjust the players in the network so that learning, and thus overall performance, is increased is critical to the preservation of the network. In the absence of such data, the inevitable bad behavior of one or more parts of the network will have one of two results. In some cases it could simply end the network experiment, which is especially likely where the remnants of an older bureaucracy exist and are looking for reasons to destroy the network. In other cases, it could lead to such a degree of specificity and control over each organization in the network that the result is really no better than an old-fashioned bureaucracy. The work is routinized, and the chief attraction of the network—its ability to innovate—is lost to the public-policy goal.

Problems with military contractors in Iraq and in the war on terror in general are indicative of the accountability problems of government by network. Outside of weapons development, the military has never really been an example of government by network. Although it has contracted out many functions from weapons development to food service, fighting—the core function of the military—has always been done by personnel in uniform. But in recent years even that has begun to change. Peter Singer, a doctoral student at Harvard, has written a dissertation, now a book called *Corporate Warriors: The Rise of the Privatized Military Industry,* in which he asserts that "The privatized military industry offers capabilities that extend across the entire spectrum of military activities, all recently limited to the state, now transferred outside it."[19] As of 2002, approximately thirty-five companies were in the war-fighting business and the range of their functions has begun to obscure the line between government and contractor. According to *New York Times* reporter Leslie Wayne: "Blurring the line between military and civilian, they provide stand-ins for active soldiers in everything from logistical support to battlefield training and military advice at home and abroad."[20]

In some senses it is inevitable that the military would drift toward a model of government by network at a point in history where the force structure, built for conventional warfare, is largely inadequate for the tasks at hand. Networks allow for flexibility and innovation, not all of it good. A privatized force allows the Pentagon to wage private wars against drug traffickers in Colombia and to train forces in countries where the international situation would not allow or welcome US forces. It also allows the Pentagon to evade limits imposed by Congress that place ceilings on the number of US soldiers that can be deployed to certain countries, and it permits private companies to use questionable interrogation techniques in prisons in Afghanistan and Iraq.

Nowhere are the accountability problems of government by network clearer than in the increasing use of contractors to do military tasks. Sometimes these contractors are used to evade congressional mandates. Private-contract soldiers are not subject to the US Code of Military Justice and yet they can be found flying helicopters and carrying arms in pursuit of US foreign-policy goals. No one really knows to whom they are accountable. Is it the United States or their contract? And when things get really hot in a combat zone, military personnel, even those in support positions, are supposed to be able to grab a gun and fight. But what if those positions are manned by civilians under contract? Are they required to fight or may they simply leave? As more and more private contractors are killed in Afghanistan and Iraq, who is responsible for their safety?

And, some military contractors, like contractors in any network, are prone to bad behavior but in this arena the bad behavior can be particularly heinous. For example, employees of DynCorp were discovered

Table 3.3   Accountability and Leadership in Government by Network

Degree of Transparency	Accountability Mechanism	Accountability versus Innovation	Management Goals	Management Pitfalls
Medium to low	Goals existing in each contract, even though they may be vague or incomplete goals and may or may not exist for the network as a whole	Medium to high levels of innovation	Understanding causality in the network and managing the parts around a goal for the entire network; defining successful network performance; analyzing elements of success and failure; weeding out bad performers and rewarding good performers	Over-regulation and/or an emphasis on process driving out innovation; overcoming political problems in replacing poor performers in the network; scandal in one part of the network dooming the entire network; networks being used to evade congressional mandates

running a sex ring in Bosnia, and MPRI won a contract to train the Croatian army after being referred to the Croatian defense minister by the Pentagon. This army then conducted Operation Storm, one of the worst episodes of "ethnic cleansing" in the region. And, as the prison scandal in Iraq unfolded it became evident that private contractors for the CIA and FBI were being used to interrogate prisoners in contradiction of the rules for such interrogations.

One of the biggest challenges for future leaders will be to determine the trade-off between greater innovation and less accountability. Table 3.3 summarizes these issues.

Government by Market

In traditional bureaucratic government, the system is transparent because there are rules and reporting requirements covering vast amounts of the government's activities. In reinvented public-sector organizations transparency is also high even though some rules and regulations are replaced by performance measures. In government by network, the transparency of the system tends to be low because it is difficult to understand both the contracts and the outcomes of a wide variety of organizations participating in the network. But in government by market transparency is even lower, since it is impossible to monitor what hundreds of companies, or thousands or even millions of individuals, are doing in response to the market—except in the aggregate. Nevertheless, government by market can be accountable. Over time the amount of some pollutant in the atmosphere can be measured and the cleanliness of the highways assessed. But the market must be allowed time to work, and accountability can only be applied to the whole, for it is almost impossible to apply it to the parts.

Government by market is a very powerful alternative to traditional bureaucracy precisely because it allows an unlimited number of individual adaptations to the achievement of the overall public good. It is therefore perfectly suited to the United States, where citizens place a high value on individual choice. And it leads to high levels of innovation, since there are few or no regimes laid out for how to comply with the market.

As we will see, the biggest challenge in government by market is creating it properly in the first place. Getting the price right, the scope right, and the information right, and making sure that the rule of law is adequate are all extremely difficult. But if they are achieved and if the market is designed properly, the primary job of the government manager is to prevent cheating and gaming. As a relevant example, in the first years after the expansion of the earned income tax credit, large-scale cheating—especially on the part of tax preparers who would "lend" money to poor people and then take their EITC refund—nearly doomed the program.[21]

One popular means of getting the earned income tax credit was to claim children that did not exist. The IRS was able to step in and tighten the requirements, thus saving the program. Those who lead a government by market, therefore have to pay constant attention to "innovations" that may or may not undercut the purpose of the market.

This is extraordinarily difficult even in the private market. For instance, in 1999, Arthur Levitt, head of the Securities and Exchange Commission (SEC), gave a speech on new order-handling rules, which required that customer-limit orders in all markets be publicly exposed and two-tier pricing eliminated. This he used as but one example of the mission of the SEC—to create "Quality Markets."[22] The spate of corporate scandals in the spring and summer of 2002 and the resulting reform legislation, called Sarbanes-Oxley after the sponsoring legislators, have illustrated the continuing need for the government to be alert to changes in the market that threaten its overall quality.

The government leader that wishes to create and manage a "quality" market in a public good will have to be every bit as vigilant against cheating and gaming the system and every bit as concerned about the quality of the information as are those regulatory agencies that monitor the private markets. The trick will be, as it is in government by network, to regulate without bleeding the networks or markets of the creativity and capacity for innovation, which are their strongest feature.

A second pitfall for government by market comes from the need to periodically adjust the pricing mechanisms. In some forms of government by market, such as the SO_2 emissions–trading system, the market takes care of the price (e.g., as more and more plants fixed their systems the price of SO_2 vouchers dropped). But in other forms of government by market, the government needs to have the political will to adjust prices. Over time a nickel on a Coca-Cola can or on a beer bottle is likely to be less of an incentive to recycling than it was in the 1970s. More important, if the price of day-care vouchers or school vouchers is allowed to get too low, it will result in fewer and fewer providers and diminished quality.

Table 3.4   Accountability and Leadership in Government by Market

Degree of Transparency	Accountability Mechanism	Accountability versus Innovation	Management Goals	Management Pitfalls
Low	Performance measured only in the aggregate and after some time has passed	High levels of innovation, since adaptation to the goal is determined individually	Preventing cheating and gaming of the market; setting prices correctly and adjusting as necessary; providing quality information that is accessible to all	Temptation to overregulate may be driving out innovation or creating opportunities for gaming; over time pricing possibly becoming obsolete and failing to achieve the public goal

Conclusion

These new and emerging forms of postbureaucratic government have their strengths and weaknesses. Each one is open to great creativity and innovation and susceptible to great cheating and stealing from the public purse. That is why it is easy to criticize the postbureaucratic state. And yet the impetus to the creation of that state, the need for innovation and creativity in the context of increasingly complex government problems, is not going away. Instead of pretending that the government will disappear or wishing that it could remain the same, those who care about the quality of governance need to concentrate on how to make the elements of the postbureaucratic state accountable without robbing it of the creativity it was designed to provide. This means that leaders in government will often need new skills in addition to courage, integrity, and a belief in the public mission—qualities that have made for good public leaders no matter what the century.

Notes

1. Paul Light, *Monitoring Government: Inspectors General and the Search for Accountability* (Washington, DC: Brookings Institution Press, 1993).

2. Bob Behn, *Rethinking Democratic Accountability* (Washington, DC: Brookings Institution Press, 2001).

3. Frank Anechiarico and James B. Jacobs (Chicago: University of Chicago Press, 1996).

4. Laurence J. O'Toole Jr., "The Implications for Democracy in a Networked Bureaucratic World," *Journal of Public Administration Research and Theory* 3 (July 1997): 449.

5. James. R. Thompson, "The Civil Service Under Clinton," *Review of Public Personnel Administration* 21, 2 (Summer 2001).

6. Vice President Al Gore and the National Performance Review, *The Best Kept Secrets in Washington* (Washington, DC: Government Printing Office, 1996).

7. The Internal Revenue Service Restructuring and Reform Act of 1998 (Public Law 105-206) contains a section called "Improvement in Personnel Flexibilities" (Section 1201), which includes civil service reforms such as pay banding, streamlined demonstration, authority and category ranking.

8. H.R. 5005, the Homeland Security Act of 2002, contains two sections that have been especially controversial. Section 9701 gives the secretary of the department authority to create a "flexible and contemporary" human resource management system. Section 763 gives management authority to transfer appropriations between accounts with only sixty days' notice to the relevant congressional committees, a provision that Senator Robert Byrd (Democrat, West Virginia) finds especially troublesome.

9. See www.ashinstitute.harvard.behavioralhealth.html.

10. Robert Stone, *Confessions of a Civil Servant: Lessons in Changing America's Government and Military* (Lanham, MD: Rowman & Littlefield, 2003).

11. Jane Fountain, *Virtual Government* (Washington, DC: Brookings Institution Press, 2001).

12. "Ex-Official Tells of Homeland Security Failures," *USA Today,* December 27, 2004.

13. Steven Kelman, "Strategic Contracting Management," *Market-Based Governance,* John D. Donahue and Joseph S. Nye, eds. (Washington, DC: Brookings Institution Press, 2002).

14. Ibid., 93.

15. Robert Agranoff and Michael McGuire, "Big Questions in Public Network Management Research," *Journal of Public Administration Research and Theory* (July 2001): 296.

16. Stephen Goldsmith and William D. Eggers, *Governing by Network: The New Shape of the Public Sector,* (Washington, DC: Brookings Institution Press, 2004), 184.

17. "Making Welfare to Work Fly," *Manhattan Institute for Policy Research,* 24 (New York: Manhattan Institute, January 2000), at www.manhattan-institute.org/html.cb 24.htm.

18. Ibid.

19. Peter Singer, *Corporate Warriors: The Rise of the Privatized Military Industry* (Ithaca, NY: Cornell University Press, 2003).

20. Leslie Wayne, "America's For-Profit Secret Army: Military Contractors Are Hired to Do the Pentagon's Bidding Far from Washington's View," *New York Times,* October 13, 2002, Section 3.

21. The earned income tax credit gives money back, through the tax system, to low-income individuals who are also raising families. It is one of the most important antipoverty programs of recent decades.

22. Arthur Levitt (chairman, US Securities and Exchange Commission), "The Changing Markets" (Speech delivered to Columbia Law School, New York, September 23, 1999).

4

The Problem with the Bureaucratic Instinct

SO FAR WE have looked at the revolution in policy implementation and laid out some ways of matching means to ends, as well as some of the accountability and leadership challenges inherent in the postbureaucratic state. To work best, the implementation tools available to both political and civil service leaders must be matched to the appropriate policy problems. In addition, the accountability mechanisms, management goals, and pitfalls must be defined and understood.

To deepen our understanding of the postbureaucratic state, we now turn to a discussion of two policy problems that will be dealt with throughout this book: welfare dependence and homeland security. These have been chosen because they are very different policy areas; they are not dealt with in the same government organizations, they are not studied by the same scholars, and they almost never appear in the same book. And yet the purpose of choosing these two very different examples is that they illustrate the need for a new way of thinking about policy implementation and the wide applicability of the models presented.

Welfare Dependence and the Problem with Bureaucratic Thinking

The most important social program of the twentieth century was, and remains so to this day, the portion of the Social Security Act of 1935 that created old-age pensions. In spite of the fact that people are increasingly worried about the financial solvency of Social Security, the old-age pension portion of the act remains one of the most popular federal government programs. The pensions never really fell prey to the problems of the bureaucratic state because from the beginning the policy goal was one that was easily routinized. People pay into the system, and when they are older the system pays them back. The bureaucracy needs to keep the

45

records and cut the checks. Since everyone gets old and nearly everyone works (or is married to a worker) the program is, at bottom, a gigantic accounting system well suited to bureaucratic routinization and has, over the years, been modernized using information technology.

Long before the term "reinvented government" was established, SSA was remaking itself as a reinvented public-sector organization. Along with DOD, it pioneered the use of computers in government in the 1960s and the use of teleservice in the 1980s. SSA was "customer focused" long before the term was in use in public administration circles.[1]

This has not been the case with some of the other portions of the Social Security Act, for instance the one that created the Aid to Dependent Children program, cash assistance to families without bread-winners or welfare. The program was based on mothers' pension pro-grams that had been in existence in most states before enactment of the legislation. The initial architects of Aid to Dependent Children expected that most of its recipients would be widows with children. Even as the program was being established it provoked debates about the "worthy" and the "unworthy" poor. In an era when mothers were not expected to work, widows with children were clearly part of the "worthy" poor, but the public and its leaders were not so accepting of other people that became eligible for aid (such as divorced and unmarried women) as the act was passed and broadened.

Thus for much of the twentieth century welfare was a political issue. The American preference for work over aid led to Depression-era programs being called "work relief" instead of cash relief. Welfare poli-cy has been subject to attacks by politicians on the right for the percep-tion that it was fostering dependence and rewarding bad behavior, and subject to attack by politicians on the left for the perception that the ben-efits were too low and programs too poorly designed to ever lift the poor out of poverty. Along the way, successive presidents and Congresses ini-tiated reform efforts to correct one or more of the misgivings about the program. Most of the efforts failed to lower welfare rolls that just seemed to keep rising regardless of economic conditions. By the late 1980s the welfare system pleased no one on the left and no one on the right. A succession of efforts to convert it into a program that offered the incentive of work had failed. Here was a classic case of a bureaucratic system that could not seem to deliver to anyone's satisfaction.

In an important book, *Welfare Realities, From Rhetoric to Reform,* two of the scholars whose work inspired the Clinton administration's welfare reform proposals—Mary Jo Bane and David Ellwood—describe the system as it existed in the early 1990s.[2] This version of the system focused almost exclusively on the process for making sure that a welfare recipient met all the legal requirements for receiving benefits and all the legal requirements for participating in related programs. Ironically, the well-intentioned welfare rights movement of the late 1960s and early 1970s exacerbated this tendency by increasing the amount of rulemaking in the system and involving the courts in an effort to achieve perfect conformity in the determination of welfare eligibility. In a detailed description of this process, Bane and Ellwood concluded the following:

> There is little in the relationship between recipients and line workers that would aid a recipient in putting together the necessary child support, child care arrangements, training and employment necessary to become self-supporting....The eligibility-compliance culture that characterizes the current welfare system contrasts sharply with what we might call a self-sufficiency culture.[3]

The eligibility-compliance culture was so powerful that it ended up distorting reforms that were designed to break out of it. For instance, in 1967 Congress, in one of many attempts to transform welfare into a program leading to work, enacted the WIN (Work INcentive) program that required welfare recipients to register for work and training. But instead of transforming the dominant culture, as Bane and Ellwood continue, WIN succumbed to it instead. "In most welfare offices WIN quickly became a paper compliance process, with clients and workers going through the motions of WIN registration, followed by a tacit understanding that neither the client nor the employment service was required to do much more."[4]

The bureaucratic imperative also ended up creating perverse incentives in the system. For instance, the federal government attempted to control the cost of welfare by paying a great deal of attention to accuracy in the determination of eligibility and by rewarding states for greater accuracy. As Bane and Ellwood pointed out, the rules governing income in addition to welfare benefits were complex. Their complexity created a paradox. Clients with extra income were more "error prone." Consequently they were called in more often and subjected to even more requests for documentation. The message sent by the welfare bureaucracy to the recipient who tried to work was clear: Don't bother; you're causing us problems. By following the bureaucratic imperative, state welfare agencies were creating a strong disincentive to work or at least a strong disincentive to report work.[5]

By the time Bill Clinton ran for president in 1992 with his famous pledge to "end welfare as we know it," the welfare system had thwarted many attempts at reform. Why? Clearly there were many reasons, but the one relevant to this argument is that earlier welfare reform efforts never really broke out of the bureaucratic model that hampered the effectiveness of the policies in the first place. As much as Congress and others tried to transform the system into one that guided clients off welfare and into self-sufficiency, the goal was not one that bureaucratic organizations could easily be expected to achieve. Unlike establishing eligibility, the goal of moving people toward work and self-sufficiency required too much innovation for traditional bureaucracy.

When Congress passed and President Clinton signed the Personal Responsibility and Work Opportunity Reconciliation Act of 1996, predictions about its future were grim indeed. The Children's Defense Fund predicted a double-digit increase in child poverty. The Urban Institute said that millions would be pushed into poverty. Senator Daniel Patrick Moynihan called it a "brutal act of social policy." Nearly a decade into its implementation none of these things has happened.

Nonetheless, the final verdict on welfare reform is yet to come. We do know that since its enactment welfare caseloads are down dramatically. "Between 1989 and 1994 national welfare caseloads rose 34 percent. Since 1994, caseload levels have undergone unprecedented declines in all states."[6] The aggregate statistics on poverty rates and the poverty rates of female-headed households tell a cautiously optimistic story. In 1993 the national poverty rate stood at 15.1 percent of the population. By 1996, when welfare reform was passed, it had dropped to 13.7 percent. Poverty rates reached a low of 11.3 percent in 2000. By 2003 they had crept up to 12.5 percent, due to the recession, but they still were not up to their 1996 rates.

A more precise measure of the effects of welfare reform is the poverty rate for households headed by women. These households had poverty rates of 38.7 percent in 1993 and 35.8 percent in 1996, when welfare reform was passed. The poverty rate for households headed by women sank to a low of 28.5 percent in the year 2000—a reflection of the robust economy of that time. By 2003 poverty rates for female-headed households had crept back up to 30 percent, still lower than their rates in either 1993 or 1996.[7]

Perhaps most important for the long-term future of the program, teen pregnancy rates have come down. In 1993 the teen pregnancy rate was 108 births per 1,000 women; in 1996, the year welfare reform was passed, it had dropped to 95.6 per 1,000 women; and by 2000 it had dropped, yet again, to 83.6 births per 1,000 women.[8] In addition to these positive figures, there is a great deal of anecdotal evidence to indicate that women who once would have been lifelong welfare recipients are now firmly incorporated into the workforce. After being a hot-button issue for so many years welfare was almost never mentioned in the 2004 presidential campaign.

Assessing causality here is a topic well beyond the scope of this book. Some poor women have been moved off welfare rolls into other government programs like SSI (Supplemental Security Income). Others are struggling in low-wage jobs and may end up no better off or even back on some other form of public assistance. It is difficult to assess the overall goal, but in the shorter term there is no doubt that after many years of trying, the welfare system has been turned into one that is more attuned to work than the previous system.

How did that happen? Why were the reforms of the 1990s able to escape the bureaucratic imperative that had hampered so many earlier reforms? Obviously policy changes in the program itself helped. The imposition of time limits on benefits meant that women could no longer expect to live a life on welfare. Other changes helped as well, such as expanded access to and funding for child support and the extension of Medicaid benefits to more of the working poor and their children. But to these changes we should add innovations in the way welfare policy was implemented.

As we have seen, for many years welfare reform was conceptualized within the bureaucratic apparatus of the state, and, not surprisingly, the reforms came up lacking. In the late 1980s and early 1990s, people who cared about poverty stopped thinking solely in terms of the welfare bureaucracy and began to try new ideas and involve new organizations. The biggest innovation, which we explore in the chapter on government by network, was to outsource almost all welfare-to-work training to a wide variety of organizations: traditional welfare offices, nonprofit organizations, for-profit organizations, and even religious organizations. The expansion of this network (presaged by the many waivers granted to states to conduct welfare-reform experiments even before passage of the bill) created exactly what our analysis predicts—a burst of creativity and innovation in helping women from welfare dependence to work. A combination of reinvented government and government by network applied to different elements of the welfare problem helped to sort the elements into new implementation modes, freeing social workers to do what they were trained to do and injecting competition and, consequently, creativity into a formerly rule-bound system.

In other words, when reformers started to break out of bureaucratic boxes and come up with new policy-implementation models for the twenty-first century, results appeared in a system that had been impervious to such results for a long time.

Failure of Bureaucratic Thinking
and the Problem of Homeland Security

Shortly after the September 11, 2001, terrorist attacks and the appointment of Pennsylvania Governor Tom Ridge as director of the newly created Office of Homeland Defense, the *New York Times* published an elaborate organization chart.[9]

More than 150 boxes, linked in a jigsaw of formal and semiformal relationships, constituted a picture of daunting complexity. One New York hostess, knowing of my experience in the federal government, thrust it into my hand as I walked into a dinner party, saying, "Is this for real?"

As the United States struggles to adapt its institutions to the challenge of terrorism, its progress may well serve as the archetype for its adaptation to many of the other complex challenges of the twenty-first century. Like getting individual women off welfare and into work, the problem of terrorism is not suited to bureaucratic routinization. After all, the terrorism problem is not in any one political jurisdiction or social entity but can be found in a loosely defined web that may span as many as sixty such. The problem exists inside and outside the United States, and therefore spans borders and bureaucratic jurisdictions. The leadership structure of terrorist organizations is ambiguous, and terrorists constantly change their methods and targets, which are likely to be random and haphazard. The solutions to the problem exist in many disparate pieces of the affected governments, all of which have other, and important, missions not concerned with terrorism. It is difficult to imagine sustaining a bureaucracy dedicated solely to a problem that is likely to be episodic.

And yet, in the years since 9/11, policymakers have continually failed to confront the fact that the government models they inherited from the twentieth century are obsolete. The natural instinct of those schooled in the bureaucracy of the past century was to try to organize the boxes on the chart into a comprehensible hierarchy. Consider, for instance, the most high-profile reforms to date: the creation of a homeland security czar, the creation of the Department of Homeland Security, and the creation of a director of national intelligence. To these we should add an idea that is talked about from time to time, which is the creation of a domestic intelligence agency that would be the US equivalent of Britain's MI5. Each of these responses illustrates how powerful the bureaucratic instinct is and how policymakers continue to believe that there is some top-down fix to deal with a problem. Let us look at each response.

Confronted with the worst ever attack on US soil, the first response of the president was to appoint a "coordinator." This was not unexpected. Confronted with twenty-first-century problems, one of the more popular responses of twentieth-century governments has been to "coordinate." "The only turf we should be worried about protecting is the turf we stand on," said Tom Ridge on his being sworn in as the new homeland defense director.

Governor Ridge's position was created by an executive order of the president to coordinate the government's homeland defense. Executive orders can be powerful instruments but they are no substitute for real legal authority and for real money, neither of which Governor Ridge had. He could "review" budgets submitted by agencies, but he could not alter them. In his first year in office he "coordinated" forty-plus different government agencies with approximately 100 staff members "borrowed" from other agencies, but he did not have the ability to make a single one of them do what he wanted.

Washington usually loves this type of high-level "coordinator" of policy. Coordination occurs at the top, makes for a good press conference, and does not require the painful process of changing the way government goes about its business. In recent years we have had a high-level coordinator of drug policy (the "drug czar"), and a high-level coordinator of AIDS policy. They both have had to borrow staff and beg for money.

But after 9/11 even the Washington establishment, usually so enthusiastic about coordination, sensed that it would be inadequate as a strategy for homeland security. Former Gen. Barry McCaffrey was the "drug czar," or director of the Office of Drug Policy, in the last years of the Clinton administration. He exchanged command of real troops in Central and South America for this job. Through sheer force of personality he made a difference, and yet this quote from him about Tom Ridge's early role comes from his own, somewhat bitter, experience. "If all [Mr. Ridge] has are five people and a black sedan, he'll be a speakers' bureau for U.S. counter-terrorism efforts and nothing more."[10]

The problem with coordination as traditionally defined is that it occurs in the cabinet room in the White House, not at the borders where terrorists are to be stopped. A coordinator can sit with the president all day long and not have an impact on what goes on within the agencies he or she coordinates. It is doubtful that the presence of a homeland security czar in the White House on September 11, 2001, would have made any difference in the utilization of the FBI field memos that described how young Arab men were taking flying lessons and that failed to reach the top of the relevant agency.

Anyone who sits in the White House is very far removed from actual operations. And that is part of the reason why Director Ridge's first seven months in office were very frustrating. At one point, Ridge was placed in the position of master of ceremonies at a press conference for all government agencies trying to respond (and not very well) to the mailing of anthrax to members of Congress and journalists. Shortly afterward he announced an alert system of color codes, which have been the butt of jokes on late-night television ever since.

In the first few months that the Office of Homeland Defense was in existence, people suggested that it be strengthened in ways they believed would give the coordination option some teeth. One of the most common suggestions was that it be given the authority to sign off on agency budgets vis-à-vis homeland defense. But, the experience of the drug czar's office, created in 1988 to oversee the fifty-some federal agencies involved in the war on drugs, offers a depressing precedent. In 1997, for the first time in the history of the statute that created the drug czar, General McCaffrey, as drug czar, exercised a provision in the law that allowed him to refuse to "certify" a line item in the Pentagon budget. This resulted in a showdown with the secretary of defense and a compromise, brokered by the president, that split the difference.[11] Since the executive branch can send only one budget to Congress at a time, disputes are always likely to be brokered by the president or by the Office of Management and Budget (OMB). Budgetary power in the coordinator's job is never final.

Giving power to a coordinator to "certify" budgets sounds impressive, but this power was used only once in the eighteen years that the drug czar's office has been in effect. The fact that its use resulted in an embarrassing news story and that it forced the need for presidential brokering mean that it is a power not likely to be used with any frequency. In addition, OMB is a small but highly effective and powerful bureaucracy. With 500 top-level civil servants and a deep sense that its mission is to integrate and implement the president's wishes, a second White House entity with budgetary authority would only sow confusion and further complicate the task of creating a coherent budget. All White House policy shops interact with OMB in the creation of a presidential budget, so creating another parallel office with budgetary authority in the White House is bound to fail.

Finally, amid rumors that Tom Ridge would leave his post out of frustration and a growing sense that its first bureaucratic response was not enough, the White House agreed to support a bill creating a cabinet-level department—The Department of Homeland Security. The idea had been advocated by two former US senators, Warren Rudman and Gary

Hart, who in March of 2000 had released the report of The United States Commission on National Security/21st Century.[12] This report got very little attention when released, but stands as one of the boldest and most creative descriptions of a major twenty-first-century problem and how the twentieth-century government was not equipped to deal with it. But, ironically, the most publicized recommendation in the Hart-Rudman report was a classically twentieth-century prescription—identifying a problem and creating a bureaucracy with the same name.

Under the Hart-Rudman plan, the centerpiece of the new agency would be the Federal Emergency Management Agency (FEMA) and the three agencies that deal with the nation's borders: the US Customs Service, the Border Patrol, and the Coast Guard. FEMA had been a free-standing agency, the Customs Service was in the Treasury Department, the Border Patrol was in the Immigration and Naturalization Service of the Justice Department, and the Coast Guard was in the Transportation Department.

Elements of the Hart-Rudman plan went a long way toward address-ing some of the major problems in this area. For instance, the situation at US borders, where for historical reasons jurisdiction was divided among several agencies, was an obvious weak spot in the new and emerging war against terror. Nevertheless, the initial instinct to create one bureaucracy to deal with a problem as broad as homeland defense was and remains, as we shall see, clearly inadequate for the task at hand.

Although the Bush administration initially rejected calls to create a Department of Homeland Security, it acquiesced in the midst of the furor that erupted over how the FBI had missed some of the more important warning signs of 9/11. But in the summer of 2002 progress in Congress on President Bush's version of the Hart-Rudman proposal ground to a halt, not over critical issues of intelligence and security but over traditional issues of bureaucracy. While the Bush administration knew it was creating a new bureaucracy, it tried to at least create a "rein-vented" organization. The proposal stumbled over just the freedom from central-control agencies that defines reinvented public-sector entities. The Bush proposal exempted the new department from laws on federal advisory committees, federal procurement laws, and many of the civil service laws encompassed by Title V of the Federal Code. In addition it allowed for the reallocation of up to 5 percent of appropriations between accounts—a major and long-sought piece of budget flexibility that engendered a filibuster in the Senate.

But the most serious objections to creating a more reinvented organ-ization came over the issue of civil service protections and unionization rights for the members of the new department. Democrats accused

Republicans of using the new department to play to their right wing by union busting; Republicans accused Democrats of playing to their left wing and ignoring national security. The issue turned out to be one of the major reasons that President Bush managed to pull Republican Senate candidates to victory in the 2002 midterm elections.

Faced with the first real sticky problem of the twenty-first century, lawmakers crept up to the threshold and then retreated into a familiar and largely irrelevant argument about unions, an argument that had the virtue of familiarity but that failed to deal with the problem. For instance, the very sticky issue of the intelligence agencies, how they were organized and how they gathered and analyzed intelligence, was missing from the debate over a department of homeland security. Had there been such a department in place on September 11, 2001, there is no guarantee that it would have been able to deal with the legal "wall" that had grown up within the FBI that served to separate foreign intelligence from criminal prosecutors. Nor are there any assurances that it would have been able to deal with many of the other problems subsequently identified in the *9/11 Commission Report* and other reports.

Creating the Department of Homeland Security was an exercise in reorganizing the boxes. That exercise was not unimportant and should, in fact, make *parts* of the problem better, although the inclusion of FEMA in the department has made parts of the problem worse.[13] But the more important problem is the boxes themselves and the ways in which they interact or fail to interact with each other. The problem of homeland defense is like many other problems we will face in the twenty-first century—it does not fit in one box. To the student of government in the twenty-first century the question is not about where the boxes fit on the chart, but how they operate and how they communicate with each other and with the society they are supposed to protect.

A third example of the bureaucratic instinct can be found in the intelligence community. As the 9/11 story unfolded policymakers were forced to confront the weakness of the US intelligence community in preventing such an attack. And while the *9/11 Commission Report* put forth a host of important recommendations for improving US intelligence capability, the proposal to create a single director of national intelligence was the recommendation that created the most public comment. It too is a powerful example of the strength of the bureaucratic instinct.

The proposal to create a national intelligence director (NID) was enacted in the Intelligence Reform and Terrorism Prevention Act of 2004. Like its predecessor, the creation of the position of homeland security czar, it was an attempt to create order among the intelligence "boxes" by giving one person control over budgets without control over operations. In spite of some talented and dedicated leadership at the top, it is a plan doomed to failure—especially the part that would have an NID attempt to influence the budget of the undersecretary of defense for intelligence. Differences between the NID and the secretary of defense would have to be brokered by none other than the president, a strategy of limited utility. It is likely that an intelligence czar would do one of two things: (1) rubber-stamp the intelligence budgets submitted by the agencies ostensibly within the agency or (2) end up in a series of fights with the secretary of defense that would ultimately have to be brokered by the president.

The same goes for "tasking" of assignments. Imagine the intelligence czar fighting to spend money on the collection of information in one arena against the secretary of defense, who would argue that intelligence was needed in another arena in order to protect US troops. It is not hard to see the intelligence czar ending up playing master of ceremonies, during a crisis, to heads of agencies that actually do real things.

Finally, the creation of a national intelligence director threatens to burden this community with the very last thing it needs—another layer of bureaucracy. But such proposals for an intelligence coordinator and department to deal with terrorism appeal to politicians. Why? Basically because it sounds large and substantial, which appeals to politicians because, well, they *sound* large and substantial. But real reform frequently has nothing to do with what politicians do. Rather, it has everything to do with reevaluating core operating procedures in this kind of organization—the culture of secrecy and the relationship between intelligence collectors (spies) and analysts. The challenge to the intelligence community is to transform itself from a bureaucracy that was pretty good at tracking the activities of the Soviet Union to an organization flexible enough to watch for trouble that is likely to originate in the most unexpected of places. A national intelligence director might be able to do so, but not without continual, strong presidential backing and working control over other agencies in the mix, which is a difficult (if not impossible) task.

The final reform proposal that has garnered attention in the years since 9/11 is the proposal to create a US version of MI5 (the British domestic spy agency, the counterpart to the foreign intelligence agency, MI6). Once again, the instinct reflects here the bureaucratic thinking of the twentieth century, which is to identify a problem and then create a bureaucracy to fix it. There is no doubt that the FBI did fail on several occasions to take steps that might have disrupted the 9/11 plot. But it is hard to see how creating a different agency, to work in parallel with the

FBI, would help this situation. Any American raised on a diet of television and movie dramas knows that the FBI and local police departments often trip all over each other, to the bad guys' advantage. And the myriad civil liberties problems that would arise from the creation of such an agency have not even been addressed.

A homeland security czar, department of homeland security, national intelligence director, and national version of MI5 illustrate the persistence of the bureaucratic instinct. For those raised on twentieth-century government the first response is the instinct to centralize power, decisionmaking, and budget authority. Yet the bureaucratic instinct is woefully inadequate for the problems of the new century because, in part, focusing on bureaucracy allows both political and government leaders to avoid the really hard work of internal reform.

This work takes place on the "front line," as it were, and is supported by Washington with the right signals, the right incentives, and the right flexibilities. This failure to operate in the front lines is especially dangerous in the war on terror. A terrorist is most likely to be caught by the cop on the beat and/or the local FBI office, not by someone in the White House arguing over budgets.

Only people who have worked in a bureaucracy can appreciate both the importance of the front line and the stifling effects of the bureaucratic system on that operational zone. For instance, in 2004 the FBI created a central counterterrorism operation at its headquarters in Washington. A former FBI agent, who was in close contact with people still in the field, questioned the efficacy of that move.

> This former agent said that from the field perspective even Mueller's [the current FBI chief] original move to centralize counter-terrorism operations at headquarters is wrongheaded. "That is fraught with peril," he said, "because it reduces field operators to pawns of headquarters and eliminates any sense of ownership which is the chief incentive that agents have to do good work. They've now taken that carrot away from thousands of agents in the field," he warned.[14]

Conclusion

In the case of welfare, reformers tried for decades to fashion reforms within the context of government as we know it and, not surprisingly, the reforms came up lacking. As we will see in greater detail in Chapter 6, the goal of transforming the traditional welfare system to one focused on work was long in the works. But it was only when welfare reformers stopped concentrating on the bureaucracy as the sole implementer and began to move to new models that these changes began to happen. In the case of homeland security, bureaucratic responses have so far dominated the reform agenda and have often obscured and/or prevented more important reforms.

Nonetheless, even though the bureaucratic instinct is alive and well in modern government, there are a wide variety of implementation models in use and under consideration. Welfare dependence and homeland security are policy areas of sufficient complexity that there is already a wide variety of implementation modes in use. By examining them we will begin to understand the contours of the postbureaucratic state.

This chapter concludes by establishing a model for the simultaneous analysis of policy and implementation. The first step in matching policy problems to implementation modes is to break down the policy problem into its component parts. The second step is to analyze pieces of the policy problem simultaneously with the implementation mode.

Table 4.1 lays out dimensions of a modern war on poverty in the twenty-first century. As we have seen, one of the basic critiques of the welfare system of the late-twentieth century revolved around the eligibility-compliance culture. After all, determining eligibility is a key government task in any benefit-granting system. The eligibility rules themselves and the way they are administered have important ramifications for the entire system, determining who can receive welfare, how easy or difficult it is to gain access to the system, and the overall cost of the system to the taxpayers.

The second category is transition to independence. For too many years policymakers and advocates for the poor tried to create systems that would, in fact, help women get jobs and be independent—only to see the systems fail and women return to welfare. Until the 1990s government activities in this arena were simply never very effective; they got subsumed by the eligibility-compliance culture or captured by the bureaucracy.

Table 4.1   Government Options for Reducing Poverty and Welfare Dependence

	Eligibility	Transition to Work	Prevention and Sustaining Independence
Reinvented Government			
Government by Network			
Government by Market			

The final category combines prevention with sustaining independence, since the same kinds of policies tend to prevent people from going on welfare in the first place and help keep them off welfare once they are independent and working. The vertical axis lists our new forms of policy implementation.

Similarly, homeland security can be broken into its various components. Like poverty reduction, homeland defense encompasses a variety of government missions. Almost everyone agrees that there is a continuum among the missions. According to retired air force Col. Randell Larsen, the continuum ranges from deterrence to prevention to preemption, on the one hand, and moves toward crisis management, consequence management, attribution, and retaliation, on the other.[15] The last four missions require government cooperation *after the fact.* Leaving aside, for a moment, the issues of attribution and retaliation, the homeland defense problem can be separated into three broad categories:

- Actions that will help prevent acts of catastrophic terrorism in the first place
- Actions that will protect Americans from terrorists by preempting the terrorists' actions
- Actions that will increase the effectiveness of the response to any terrorist act that does occur

These are reflected in the boxes across the top of Table 4.2.

The vertical axis of Table 4.2 shows even more government options that exist to reform or replace bureaucratic government. It encompasses five options available to policymakers. The first option is, of course, the

Table 4.2   Government Options to Achieve Homeland-Defense Missions

	Prevention	Protection	Response
Incremental Change			
Reinvented Government			
Government by Network (public)			
Government by Network (public & private)			
Government by Market			

most straightforward and probably the easiest, which is to make incremental changes to already existing programs. A great deal can be done to simply strengthen functions and agencies that already exist. The second row in Table 4.2 consists of reinvented government's public-sector organizations. It includes the changes that can be made to existing bureaucracies by reorganizing them, freeing them from obsolete central-control mechanisms, changing the legal context and administrative cultures in which they operate, or using new technologies to increase their effectiveness. The third row consists of options that involve creating and managing networks that consist entirely of public-sector organizations, while the fourth row consists of networks that involve both public- and private-sector organizations. The final row consists of the markets that government might want to create to meet some of the objectives in homeland defense.

The following chapters illustrate how the new frameworks for implementing government policy laid out in Chapter 2 can be applied to national problems. They are not meant to be a comprehensive set of actions for either reducing welfare dependence or improving homeland security. Given how fluid real public-policy problems are, no book could ever capture the range of actions either being done or that should be done at any given time.

Rather, they are meant to illustrate a new way of thinking about the dimensions of a policy problem and how to match the dimensions to an appropriate new form of government. The challenge of twenty-first century government will be to create effective portfolios of actions that incorporate reinvented public-sector organizations, government by network, and government by market.

Notes

1. See "Ruthless with Time and Gracious with People? Teleservice at the Social Security Administration" (Cambridge, MA: KSG Case CRI-96-1338).
2. Mary Jo Bane and David T. Ellwood, *Welfare Realities: From Welfare to Reform* (Cambridge, MA: Harvard University Press, 1994).
3. Ibid., 7.
4. Ibid., 21.
5. Ibid., 126.
6. Jo Ann G. Ewalt and Edward T. Jennings, Jr., "Administration, Governance and Policy Tools in Welfare Policy Implementation," *Public Administration Review* 64 (July/August 2004).
7. "Poverty Status of People by Family Relationship, Race and Hispanic Origin, 1959–2003," in Carmen De Navas-Walt, Bernadette D. Proctor, and Robert J. Mills, *Income, Poverty and Health Insurance Coverage in the United States: 2003, Current Population Reports Consumer Income P60-226*

(Washington, DC, US Department of Commerce, US Census Bureau, August 2004), Table B-1.

8. Alan Guttmacher Institute, "U.S. Teen Pregnancy Statistics" (New York, February 19, 2004).

9. "Disputes Erupt on Ridge's Needs for his Job," *New York Times,* November 4, 2001.

10. Interview with Katie Couric, "Today Show," September 24, 2001.

11. "McCaffrey, Cohen Settle Drug War Budget Dispute," *Washington Post,* December 13, 1997.

12. *Road Map for National Security: Imperative for Change,* United States Commission on National Security/21st Century, March 15, 2001.

13. A consensus about why FEMA failed to deliver aid in the aftermath of Hurricane Katrina is emerging. It points to disintegration in FEMA's capacity as a result of being included in the Department of Homeland Security. See, for instance, "Brown's Turf Wars Sapped FEMA's Strength, Director Who Came to Symbolize Incompetence in Katrina Predicted Agency Would Fail," *Washington Post,* December 23, 2005.

14. "The Survivor," *National Journal,* August 20, 2004.

15. Quoted in Paul Mann, "Technology Threat Urged Against Mass Weapons," *Aviation Week and Space Technology,* December 4, 2000, 64.

5

The Reinvented Public Sector

THE GRADUAL EVOLUTION of the bureaucratic state into a more modern form initially led some to conclude that "governance without government is becoming the dominant pattern of management for advanced industrial democracies."[1] In a 1995 issue of *Daedalus,* the words "diminished," "defective," and "hollow" were applied to the contemporary state.[2] Others have written about "governance" replacing "government" as the modus operandi of democratic societies.[3] As early as the 1970s Harlan Cleveland wrote that "the American people want less government and more governance," a sentiment that sums up the paradoxical behavior and attitudes of the public toward government in the past thirty or forty years.[4] For a while it was fashionable to assert that, in the age of information and globalization, the state would simply "wither away." But the example of so many failed and disintegrating states and the human misery that inevitably accompanies them has made discussion of statelessness considerably less fashionable.

It is now clear that much of the public's business will continue to be done through public-sector organizations, populated with public-sector employees. However, it is equally clear that these organizations have already begun to operate in ways designed to overcome what the conservative author James Pinkerton has called the "bugs" in the bureaucratic operating system (BOS).[5] "No software is trouble free;" said Pinkerton, "over time, it accumulates Bugs, like lint in a belly button."[6]

Pinkerton outlines five bugs that plague the BOS, and they are worth repeating here, since they synthesize so much of the criticism (both scholarly and popular) of modern bureaucracy. First is Peterism (named for the Peter Principle), the observation that, over time, people will rise to the level of their own incompetence. One of the hallmarks of most modern public-sector bureaucracies has been that, over time, efforts to ensure competence and protect civil servants from political cronyism end up creating systems in which it is very difficult to fire people. In the US government nearly everyone gets merit raises and nearly everyone gets above-average evaluations.

The second bug Pinkerton identifies is Parkinsonism, a reference to Parkinson's law about work expanding to fill the time allotted. For instance, at the beginning of the twentieth century the number of major ships in the British Navy fell by 67 percent, but during the same period the number of admiralty staff members rose by 78 percent.[7] At the turn of the nineteenth century, when one half of all Americans lived on farms, the US Department of Agriculture (USDA) had 2,019 employees; today only one in forty Americans live on farms, but the USDA has more than 100,000 employees. It is well known that bureaucracies take on new tasks to stay in business. A famous political scientist once wrote a provocative book titled *Are Government Organizations Immortal?*[8] The answer was yes.

The third bug in the operating system is oligarchism, named after the "iron law of oligarchy": that is, someone has to be in charge and the ruling class exists to perpetuate its own power. As examples, Pinkerton refers to another conservative thinker, Irving Kristol, who identified as the "new class" people who make their career in the expanding public sector. The power of this new class is such that Pinkerton concludes, "the biggest obstacle to change in the public sector is the public sector itself."[9] For Pinkerton, the most glaring example of this bug is the strength of public-employee unions and the power they have had, especially in big US cities at the end of the twentieth century, to elect their own bosses and to resist change.

The fourth bug in the operating system Pinkerton refers to is Olsonism, after the famous theorist Mancur Olson. Olson argued that the accretion of special interests will bury economic growth and that countries "that have had democratic freedom of organization without upheaval or invasion the longest will suffer the most from growth-repressing organizations and combinations."[10] Pinkerton argues that extensive tax breaks for the very rich, Social Security and Medicare for the middle class, and welfare and Medicaid for the poor all result in a system where all are organized around maintaining their particular piece of the state.

The fifth bug Pinkerton identifies is "information infarction" or the tendency in hierarchical organizations for information to travel down the chain of command but not up. This means that the leaders of the bureaucracy become more and more removed from the important information coming to the organization from below. The bureaucracy cannot possibly know all relevant information, which led cybernetics pioneer Norbert Wiener to conclude that "the State is stupider than most of its components"—a statement that was sadly true vis-à-vis the state pre 9/11.[11]

Taken all together, Pinkerton's "bugs" in the BOS encompass the late twentieth-century criticism of modern bureaucracy, which has been heard in the halls of Congress, on the political campaign trail, on late-night television shows, and in local diners and truck stops. If current citizens were getting more and more unhappy with their governments, it could be that they were reacting to government organizations that seemed to get bigger, more stupid, and more distant from the citizens with every day. No wonder that, in spite of all the progress the US government had made in the twentieth century, Ronald Reagan could come to power in 1980 declaring that "government is the problem, not the solution." By 1996 and 1997 a Democratic president and a British Labour Party prime minister would be declaring the need for a new "third way" in government and politics.[12]

The "bugs" in the BOS explain why reinvented public-sector organizations are at the heart of so many government reform movements currently in vogue around the world.[13] Stripped to its essence, reinvented government is entrepreneurial. Another way to look at it is that reinvented government is bureaucratic—but without all the things that made government so irritating to the citizens of information-age economies. Reinvented government is run as much like a private-sector business as possible; the literature and practice of reinvented government is replete with praise for competition, flexibility, employee empowerment, and customer service. This sort of government has reformed, or even shed, civil service and has reformed centralized procurement. As well, it has adopted performance goals, using bonuses to reward its workers and placing a premium on service to the citizen and on productivity.

Reinvented government, however, is still government. But it is government shorn of many of its public-sector trappings, especially the rigid budget rules, personnel rules, and procurement rules that restrict government managers and that are unusual, if not unheard of, in the private sector.[14] The British government was one of the first to put these theories into action with the 1988 publication of "Improving Management in Government: The Next Steps," written under the leadership of Sir Robin Ibbs. Out of this report came the creation of "next-steps" agencies or executive agencies. These were to be public-sector agencies without public-sector trappings. Next-steps agencies were to be run by CEOs hired from inside or outside the civil service on a performance contract basis and who were to be offered the potential for large bonuses. The agencies would have more control over their budget, personnel, and other management systems. The heads of these agencies would negotiate a "framework" agreement between their organizations and the relevant cabinet minister. And, perhaps the most important break with the past was that the heads of these agencies could be fired for not living up to their performance agreements.

By 1997, 130 British agencies had been set up under the next-steps framework and accounted for about 75 percent of the British civil service.[15] In just over ten years of operation, next-steps agencies (now called executive agencies) could boast a considerable record of accomplishments: improvements in the processing of passport applications, savings in "running costs" (administrative costs) in the National Health Service (NHS) Pensions Agency, improvements in waiting times in the NHS, and reductions in per unit costs at the Patent Office.[16] In separating policymaking from service delivery and compliance functions, the British government was asserting that when it came to implementation there were few, if any, management differences between the public and the private sectors.

Characteristics of Reinvented Public-Sector Organizations

As the next-steps agencies showed, government reform in the postbureaucratic age involves strategies borrowed from the private sector. Critics of bureaucratic modernization like to point out that the public sector is different, and that because it is different it should not borrow from the private sector. Still, as we shall see, many of the strategies borrowed from the private sector are borrowed in the service of traditional public-sector goals. Following is a list of the most common strategies used to create reinvented public-sector organizations:

- downsizing and technology combine to reform government operations so as to enhance productivity;
- attention to service delivery increases;
- the bureaucracy's central control mechanisms are reformed and performance measures are introduced in their place, with particular emphasis on the incentive structures of front-line employees;
- regulatory functions are reformed, and the emphasis on enforcement is augmented by a renewed emphasis on compliance;
- an ethos of innovation, experimentation, and cross-agency work replaces the ethos of rule making.

Productivity

Downsizing is often a key element in the effort to create a reinvented public-sector organization. In the near term it is often associated with a fiscal crisis, but in the long term it is one of the most important adaptations the public sector can make as it crawls out from under bureaucratic organizations and into the information age. While "downsizing" may be a dirty word, "productivity" is not. Yet the two are inseparable. In the traditional bureaucratic state the notion of productivity was seldom, if ever, applied to government. But in the last decade of the twentieth century, information technology led a revolution in productivity so profound that it could not help but affect the public sector. For instance, SSA, which has to keep earnings records of millions of Americans and then determine benefits for them when they reach retirement age, has been using telephones, computers, and the Internet to prepare for when members of the baby boom generation retire. SSA does not anticipate hiring thousands of more people to deal with all the coming retirements—it anticipates using technology to improve the productivity of the workforce.

In this nation, public-sector downsizing was most successful when it took place in the context of organization reengineering that focused on the front-line activities of an agency. For instance, early in the Clinton administration, Undersecretary of Labor Tom Glynn discovered that the personnel office was using a hiring process that entailed 113 steps. By reengineering the process down to a more reasonable number of steps he was able to save full-time equivalents (FTEs) and use those positions to hire more federal Occupational Safety and Health Administration (OSHA) inspectors, who performed the critical front-line job of inspecting plants for safety violations. This ideal public-sector downsizing cut bureaucracy and enhanced front-line activities (though, in reality downsizing in the public sector, as in the private sector, often results in getting rid of the wrong people).

Downsizing of government has been going on around the world, often at the insistence of development banks, which have tended to tie cuts in the public sector to aid or loan guarantees. A recent survey of government-reform movements in the world's 123 largest countries found that 43 percent of the countries studied (i.e., 41 countries) had undergone a public-sector downsizing, and that in 13 of those countries the downsizing amounted to more than 25 percent of the workforce.[17] A study of the size of the public sector in the world has found that after years of growth, the public sector is actually shrinking or remaining stable in most countries.[18]

More important, however, than the actual size of the public-sector workforce is its distribution. Given the dictates of the development banks in recent years, it surprises most people to learn that the richest countries in the world have the most government employees per capita. However, the richest countries in the world have most of their government employees employed on the front lines of the government—as teachers, police officers, and public health officials. This is not the case in many developing countries: in some the entire government workforce is employed in the capital city with no local government employees at all.[19]

We can draw two lessons from experience with downsizing. The first is that in reinvented public-sector organizations productivity matters. The message from the American public, seconded by the publics in other advanced nations around the world, has been pretty clear: they do not want less government, only the same government at lower cost.[20] The second lesson is that the distribution of public-sector employees is critical to the most effective governments. Governments that spend their entire budget on central-government employees in capital cities are not as effective as those that spend most of their money on employees on the front lines of government.

In the public sector, as in the private sector, information technology is key to downsizing and increased productivity. Most modern governments use the Internet to one degree or another. In fact a UN survey found that, out of the 190 member nations, fully 89 percent had a presence on the World Wide Web.[21] However, most of those Web pages were static; only seventeen countries had Web pages that were "transactional," meaning that citizens could use the Web to conduct their business with the government.

The fact that the public sector is a monopoly means that it has not had the same incentives that the private sector has to push the use of new information technology to transform the organization. Most government websites report relatively low use. Fears about adequate privacy, the lingering digital divide between citizens with access to the Internet and those without, and the failure of many governments to really push traffic to the Internet contribute to low use. The latter fact means that many public-sector organizations have yet to use the Internet to save money and to wipe out their back-office operations (as happened in the private financial sector in the United States and other first world countries). Clearly a reinvented public-sector organization of the future will need to use information technology to increase flexibility, citizen responsiveness, and productivity.

Two private-sector concepts, downsizing and productivity, can serve public ends by providing a level of government at no extra cost; by freeing less essential government employees for more essential government work, and by using technology to lower costs.

Service Delivery

The second characteristic of reinvented public-sector organizations is that they try to orient themselves to effective service delivery. This concept had its roots in Great Britain where, in 1991, Prime Minister John Major initiated the Charter Mark program. This program, based on ten service-oriented criteria, awarded the Charter Mark to government agencies for excellence in service to the citizen. Similarly, in 1994 President Clinton issued an executive order directing all federal agencies that dealt with the public to establish and publish customer-service standards. These programs have spread rapidly around the world and are hallmarks of reinvented public-sector organizations. Where they have driven downsizing and reorganization built around the goals of service, they have gone a long way toward fixing the bugs inherent in the old bureaucracy.

But the difficulty in enforcing a service mentality in government is that so much of government is a monopoly. For instance, no other entity can give out passports and drivers' licenses. Therefore, the challenge is to create some sort of market proxy (like the British Charter Mark or federal Customer Service Standards) that serves to push the public monopoly into adopting some of the behaviors that exist in competitive private-sector organizations.

Service delivery has also been transformed by forcing government providers to look at the citizen as the center of the system. In Great Britain, this has led to an emphasis on individual choice and on "joined-up" government where, in order to really improve outcomes, bureaucratic departments need to cooperate in the needs of the citizen. "For example, under the Government's 14-19 reforms, young people will be able to choose from a wider range of vocational and academic programmes. This will necessitate more collaboration between local institutions...."22

The Clinton administration's National Performance Review received nonstop criticism from defenders of the traditional bureaucracy over the use of the word "customer" instead of "citizen." Yet no one ever debated the goal of treating citizens as if they were the valued customers of a well-run business. So the leadership of the National Performance Review continued to use the word "customer" for it was the only way we knew of conveying to the bureaucracy how citizens ought to be treated. Once again, it is a private-sector concept in the service of a public-sector goal.

Performance

As public-sector leaders attempted to cope with the need to govern in an antigovernment environment, they began to develop measures of public-sector performance. The incentive for these measures was twofold. Lacking a profit-or-loss statement, government leaders needed an objective measure of how they were doing. In addition, much of the public administration literature of the 1990s, especially Michael Barzelay's book on Minnesota and David Osborne and Ted Gaebler's *Reinventing Government,* stressed the appealing notion of a grand bargain in which the traditional accountability and control mechanisms of the bureaucracy would be traded for accountability to enhanced performance.

In 1993, the US Congress passed the Government Performance and Results Act (GPRA) that began the process of establishing performance measures for all activities in the federal government. The Clinton administration enthusiastically adopted the GPRA, even speeding up its implementation, and the Bush administration expanded on the GPRA through the award-winning Performance Assessment Rating Tool (PART) program mentioned earlier. There now exists an extensive system of performance measurement in all US federal agencies.

In an attempt to get at the central-control problem in another way, the US government took a page from the British experience and in 1996 introduced the notion of performance-based organizations (PBOs). These organizations were to be modeled on the next-steps agencies in the degree of managerial discretion allowed. But the US political system proved more resistant to reform than the British or the New Zealand systems. Each PBO required statutory changes and the approval of congressional committees often influenced by groups with vested interests in the status quo. By the end of the Clinton administration, only three PBOs had been enacted: the Student Loan Program at the Department of Education, the Patent and Trademark Office, and the Air Traffic Organization of the FAA. Other attempts at PBOs such as the attempt to turn the post exchanges on military bases into more modern entities fell prey to the internal politics of the bureaucracy—especially the central-control organizations that argued that they were preserving the president's constitutional prerogatives.[23] In spite of the attractiveness of PBOs, both scholars and practitioners have concluded that they are easier to enact in parliamentary democracies.[24]

Performance measurement has been used more successfully at the state and local levels than at the federal level. In the early 1990s, the city of New York, under the leadership of Mayor Rudy Giuliani and Police Chief William Bratton, began a police-reform movement that has transformed policing in the United States and throughout the world. Called Comstat, the system used crime statistics, broken down by precinct, to revolutionize the incentive structure of the New York Police Department (NYPD) from crimes caught and prosecuted to crimes prevented. Precinct captains were regularly summoned before the NYPD leadership, and were held accountable for any increase in crime in their districts. Thus the leadership of the NYPD was able to learn and catalog best practices from around the city, which they then transferred to individual captains during their reporting sessions.[25]

The use of crime statistics combined with accountability and organizational learning came to result in the lowest crime rates in New York City in decades. (The Comstat model was later applied to human services through a program called Jobstat that allowed officials to monitor the performance of their twenty-seven job centers.)[26]

Since then, the Comstat model has been applied to other government organizations around the country and the world. For instance, in Baltimore an innovative mayor, Martin O'Malley, developed an entire set of measures to guide city government (called "Citistat"). And in Washington, DC, Mayor Anthony Williams, in an attempt to rescue the city from even more federal takeover measures, instituted a comprehensive performance management program.

In reinvented public-sector organizations, performance measures are essential means of replacing the antiquated accountability measures often enshrined in the central-control mechanisms of traditional bureaucracy. Among the most criticized are centralized civil service systems that separate hiring and firing from the work of management. At the federal level, the civil service law has been chipped away in a series of agency-level reform measures. But in 1996 the state of Georgia got rid of its civil service system in what Jonathan Walters has called "the most sweeping frontal assault on civil service ever attempted in any state in the United States."[27] Leadership from Governor Zell Miller was important, as was the following story—the proverbial straw that broke the camel's back.

As Georgia prepared for the 1996 Olympics, it wanted to create a fleet of roving tow trucks that could quickly clear traffic accidents and other breakdowns on the highways. However, there was no job classification in the Georgia civil service system for a truck driver who was, essentially, a trouble-shooter. When the department of transportation asked the state's merit system to develop a new job classification so that these drivers could be hired, the department was told that it could not possibly be done until some time after the 1996 Summer Olympics. Shortly thereafter the civil service system of Georgia was scrapped, due in no small measure to the inflexibility of this particular bureaucratic operating system.

The promise of performance measurement is that it will reorient government agencies away from rules and toward problems. Performance measures are now standard fixtures in many reinvented public-sector organizations. But, as is the case with much of the "new public management," performance measures do not guarantee good performance. FEMA got relatively decent marks from the Bush administration's PART rating program in the year before it failed so spectacularly in New Orleans. One of the administration's early successes has been the No Child Left Behind federal legislation that called for states to measure school outcomes and have students be offered the choice of another school if their own was found wanting. But the absence of alternative schools convenient to parents has meant that the legislation has not had the impact it was hoped it would.

Both the Clinton and the Bush administrations have been enthusiastic supporters of performance measurement, but, so far, poor performance has not been linked to any significant consequences for federal agencies. Even the post-Katrina FEMA remains intact and funded (though there are a large number of reform proposals extant). Congress, which created and passed the GPRA in the first place, has not seemed very interested in performance measurement.

This is a conundrum to which I will return in the final chapter. Suffice it to say that while performance measures have been transforming the internal operations of many executive-branch agencies, they have not been used by legislatures to hold the agencies accountable.

Regulation

Much of what government does is regulatory in nature, and the 1990s saw the beginnings of significant reform in that arena as well. Reinvented public-sector organizations that perform regulatory functions need to strike the proper balance between encouraging compliance by working with those they regulate and retaining the ability to prosecute those who refuse to comply. To developing countries fighting corruption and struggling to establish the rule of law the movement from enforcement to compliance sounds like an invitation to even more corruption and it is therefore probably not applicable. However, in countries where the rule of law is effective, there are huge gains to be made in the ultimate goals of regulatory policy by moving to include a greater emphasis on compliance.

One of the clearest and earliest examples of this change came at OSHA. In Maine, OSHA officials had won prize after prize for the enforcement of penalties against violations of workplace safety. Yet even as they won prizes for enforcement they found that injury and fatality rates at the workplaces in Maine were increasing. This led the OSHA officials in Maine to design a series of innovations that were to become agencywide policy—innovations that focused on helping companies and workers and their unions understand and comply with workplace safety rules and regulations.[28]

OSHA front-line inspectors had faced an incentive system based solely on the enforcement model, which produced less than stellar success. The same thing was happening at the IRS when Charles Rossotti took over as the service's commissioner. In a series of congressional hearings in the summer of 1997, many sympathetic US citizens, such as elderly widows who had lost their husbands, testified to the IRS inspectors' heavy-handed tactics. It turned out that the inspectors, like those with OSHA, had been rewarded according to the number of cases in which they recovered back taxes. Not surprisingly, they went after the easy cases to keep their numbers up. Rossotti changed the system to one where enforcement was organized around "customer groups" (e.g., individuals, small businesses). In addition, he found that the single biggest problem in the tax system did not even have a place on the organization chart: people who did not pay taxes. And so he created a piece of the organization to deal with noncompliers.[29]

The movement from enforcement to compliance has taken place in the environmental area as well, but these and other reinvention stories, while generally successful, are not without the controversy common to all efforts to create modern regulatory enterprises. From the labor unions that care about the work of OSHA, to the government watchdogs that worry about overall tax revenues, to the environmentalists who care about the work of the EPA, the movement to greater compliance looks and feels as if it is a movement away from prosecuting evildoers in the workplace or in nature. And yet, as Kevin Phillips's best-selling *The Death of Common Sense* illustrates, a mature regulatory state, after years of reliance on an adversarial legal edifice for the accomplishment of its goals becomes so bound up in its own rules and regulations that it defies common sense and contributes to the widespread distrust of government discussed in Chapter 1.

No wonder that reinvented public-sector organizations involved in regulation need to reorient themselves toward compliance. Whether this works or not depends on the establishment of measures that actually reflect what the public wants—for instance, lower injury rates or cleaner air. But to those accustomed to the old ways of doing business, the movement toward encouraging greater compliance can often look like a decision to let the "bad guys" off the hook.

Innovation

Finally, reinvented public-sector organizations will need to foster a new ethos of innovation and experimentation in government. In the Clinton-Gore years two programs, the Hammer Award Program and the

Reinvention Laboratory program, served to reward innovation. The first was for teams of civil servants who, in the words of Vice President Gore, "created a government that worked better and cost less." The second program designated certain subsections of departments or agencies as "reinvention laboratories" and gave them the psychological freedom and the political protection needed to innovate. In Great Britain the Charter Mark has become a coveted award in the bureaucracy. This award has been around long enough so that, even though the award itself does not engender much coverage, the revocation of the award has become a major news story, and one to be avoided (as happened when British Gas lost its Charter Mark). Even state governments, such as Minnesota's, have experimented with innovation centers that foster and sometimes even fund state government innovation.

Still, continuous innovation runs against the public sector grain. In contrast to the private sector where constant change in the market is taken as a given, the public sector has been accustomed to a greater degree of stability. In Great Britain, one of the world's leaders in government innovation, one front-line worker told Prime Minister Tony Blair, "So Prime Minister, let me get on with it, let me experiment, without pulling the rug out from under me in the next eighteen months."[30] Moments later the prime minister responded with the following warning that "it's not only the private sector that is buffeted by those changes," referring to the fast pace of change in a globalized world and the need for public-service systems designed to continually improve and change.

In addition, reinvented governments need to value cross-agency work. The dominant culture of the US government has been to reward consistent loyalty to only one agency. In spite of attempts in the mid-1970s to reform civil service to create a leadership cadre that could move from agency to agency, thus gaining government-wide experience, cross-agency service is rare. But globalization has a way of making the jurisdictional boundaries of old-fashioned bureaucracies meaningless.

There is the contemporary experience of the US State Department. In the days when Ben Franklin and Thomas Jefferson represented the new United States in Paris, relations with other countries were under the sole control of the department. It stayed that way for many years. But after World War II, more and more government entities have been finding that they need to do business abroad. In many US embassies and consulates employees of the State Department are outnumbered by FBI or DEA agents and Commerce Department, Agriculture Department, and DOD employees—to name a few. Relationships between the US military and those of other governments are now so extensive that these personnel "often have more active contact with foreign officials than do people from any other U.S. agency, including the State Department."[31]

The State Department has been concerned about this for some time. As Graham Allison and Peter Szanton wrote, "The Department's own principal complaint has been that extraneous actors were crowding the foreign policy stage. If they could not be removed, State at least wanted the lead role among them."[32] In a well-run embassy or consulate, the ambassador has to make a team out of disparate employees over whom he or she has no real power.

However, in the late 1980s the Pentagon unwillingly became the leading example in the US government of how to break down agency barriers. Prompted by a series of military embarrassments—especially the failure of the US military mission to rescue the Iranian hostages in April 1980—Senators Sam Nunn and Barry Goldwater took the lead in creating a series of reforms at DOD designed to reduce interservice rivalries and create the kinds of unified commands essential to battlefield victories. Central to this concept was the concept of cross-training. Congress forced a reluctant military to promote officers only if they had engaged in some sort of job in another service. The goal was to break down the institutional walls and create greater understanding of other services. As the result of the Goldwater-Nichols reforms, members of the separate services were forced to train in another service *as a condition of advancement in their own service.* In the reinvented public organizations of the future, cross-agency service will be something to be sought out and valued.[33]

Reinvented Government in Practice

As this new way of implementing policy became more widespread, many scholars expressed fears about where it was going, mainly that somehow this new philosophy would undercut the rule of law.[34] However, as many a practitioner of entrepreneurial or reinvented government knows, the law itself is often very flexible—but the administrative application of the law, over time, may introduce a degree of rigidity into the implementation of a program, seriously impeding the program's original intent. Considine and Lewis set out to ask about the behavior of civil servants on the front lines of these reforms. Somewhat to their surprise they found out that civil servants in newer, "reformed" organizations did not differ from other civil servants when it came to the importance of rules in their work. They conclude that "it also is possible that rules are always so much a part of even the most flexible public programs that they do no more than define the parameters of action and fail to define actual work strategies."[35]

But the success of reinvented government depends, as outlined in Chapter 2, on its proper application to policy problems. Thus the next half of this chapter shows when and how reinvented public-sector organizations can help solve some aspects of the two policy problems, welfare dependence and homeland security, that serve as our examples.

Applying Reinventing Government to the Problem of Welfare Dependence

Eligibility. As we saw in Chapter 4, eligibility dominated the old welfare system to the exclusion of everything else. But determining eligibility for government benefits is central to the policy and the budgetary functions of government. Deciding who gets into a welfare system and who gets excluded is a major governmental function. People in the government care about this because slight changes in eligibility can have big impacts on federal, state, or even local budgets. For instance, changes in eligibility for the Supplemental Security Income (SSI) program, which is funded with federal dollars, caused states experiencing fiscal problems to move as many children as they could from the old Aid to Families with Dependent Children (AFDC) into the SSI program.[36] In addition to governments, advocates for the poor care about eligibility because they want the programs to reach as many of those in need as possible. A recent study found that children were more likely to be enrolled in State Children's Health Insurance (SCHIP) programs if the bureaucratic hurdles were lowered and the program was administered as a Medicaid expansion, asset tests were removed, and eligibility presumed.[37]

Eligibility determination is one part of the welfare program that should and has remained in the public sector. However, it has undergone dramatic changes in the past two decades—changes that began before the enactment of the 1996 welfare reforms and are good examples of reinvented government. Mostly these changes involve reengineering and streamlining the eligibility process so that a poor people can become eligible for the full variety of government programs.

For instance, Merced County, California, found in 1995 that the process of determining eligibility in a single welfare office involved more than 700 paper forms. The complexity of the forms allowing access to five government programs meant that "a client in need might have to complete up to 30 pages of application forms and be interviewed by two or more workers. By the end of the 1980s, clients had to wait 30 to 45 days to be notified about the status of their benefits."[38] Merced County workers got together and redesigned the application process so that AFDC, Medicaid, Foster Care, the food stamp program, and refugee assistance could be determined in one step and in a one-page application. When the program was fully operational it had achieved the enormous increases in productivity that are characteristic of reinvented governments: the county managed to handle an increased caseload (47 percent greater) with a reduced staff, clients got their benefits determined in one to four days, hundreds of forms were eliminated, and training time for workers was cut.[39]

Similar achievements in productivity in welfare offices occurred in Los Angeles County, where the creation of the Los Angeles Eligibility, Automated Determination Evaluation and Reporting System (LEADER) incorporated all the complex rules and regulations for California's different welfare systems into one system. As a result, the county can notify clients of their eligibility within hours (it used to take a month) and the new system is expected to save the county $83 million a year.[40]

Many counties and states were using information technology to reinvent their welfare agencies even before passage of the federal 1996 welfare-reform law, but with its passage the need to create systems that could integrate programs and track how long a person was on welfare (the law mandated a five-year time limit on the receipt of welfare) became even more urgent. By 2000, a technology publication was estimating that information technology expenditures for human services would reach $9.6 billion by 2005, since nearly half of the states were planning changes to their eligibility systems.[41] And an overview of state reform efforts found that forty states were implementing new client-tracking and accountability systems and thirty-nine states were implementing new program accessibility and certification systems. [42]

Classic reinvented government strategies, borrowed from the private sector, have helped change welfare administration in ways that help the system achieve some of its goals. Clients are more likely to receive the full range of benefits they are eligible for if the eligibility process can be reduced to one step and the computer can reconcile differing eligibility criteria. The sheer complexity of the application process and the differences in eligibility criteria had been major barriers to entry, often keeping eligible clients away from the services they needed. In addition, the use of information technology has helped to reduce errors and reduce fraud—a subject we will cover later.

But for those reformers interested in the success of the system, the major reason to use reinvented government to reform eligibility was to free social workers to do what they were trained to do: help people deal with their problems. But the study cited above, which documented extensive reengineering of welfare eligibility, found that although eligibility reforms were being pursued in thirty-nine states, the role of the caseworker had changed in only eighteen. Does this mean that eligibility reform failed to free social workers for the needs of their clients?

At first glance the answer is yes. A study of front-line workers in welfare agencies, published in 2004, six years after the reforms, found that "workers in local welfare systems consider goals related to eligibility determination to be more important to their agencies than goals related to either the employment or welfare deterrence/behavior modification goals of recent welfare reforms."[43] If, as we saw in Chapter 4, the old welfare system was weighed down by a bureaucratic culture that emphasized compliance with rules over assistance to poor people, what, if anything, has changed? The biggest change is the realization that public-sector bureaucracies are probably not the best organizations to do the highly personal work of employment counseling. The study of front-line workers, cited above, showed that their work was to determine eligibility because in ten out of the eleven sites studied, promoting employment was assigned to agencies other than the welfare office! In other words, rather than pretending that government workers could deal with bureaucratic, rule-driven parts of the job *and* with personal counseling parts simultaneously, the two functions have, by and large, been divided in the new welfare system.

In Chapter 6, we will look at the system for getting welfare mothers into work, since it is a good example of government by network. But for our purposes it is instructive to note that, in the case of welfare reform, the public sector retained and reinvented that portion of the process it should and could do, and decided to handle the other parts of the job through nonprofit and for-profit organizations specializing in employment counseling.

Electronic transfer of benefits. In addition to information technology used to streamline the eligibility process, other examples of how reinvented government has transformed the welfare world are innovations designed to move from paper forms (e.g., checks, food stamps) to electronic forms of benefits such as "smart cards."

Reinvented government began to change benefit transfers in the mid-1980s in Ramsey County, Minnesota, when the First Bank of St. Paul became the third local bank to cancel its account with the county welfare office. Like the two other banks before it, First Bank of St. Paul determined that long lines of poor people trying to cash their welfare checks on the same day was not good for the rest of its business. In

1987, when Ramsey County contracted with First Texas Financial Corporation to develop an electronic benefits transfer program for the county, both entities had entered uncharted waters. First Texas (later named TransFirst) saw the market potential in public-assistance programs and offered the county very generous terms so that the bank could learn how to develop software packages for public-assistance programs—and retain the proprietary rights over any new software created.

The Ramsey County experience was ultimately successful and offered unexpected advantages in the areas that governments care about most: saving money and countering fraud. When the Clinton administration came into office in 1993, a civil servant at OMB offered the newly created National Performance Review a plan to turn the entire food stamp program into an electronic benefits program, using the Ramsey County experience (and the experiences of a few other pioneers) as a guide. The vice president and his staff jumped on the program because it promised huge savings, a reduction in fraud, and greater security and dignity for the recipients of food stamps. But first the government had to deal with Regulation E of the banking laws, which limited the liability of any credit card holder to $50 if the credit card was stolen. Applying Regulation E to the welfare population could have cost federal, state, and local governments millions of dollars. In 1995, Congress passed a law that excluded certain welfare benefits from Regulation E, thus clearing the way for the benefits to be delivered through use of a credit card.

The implementation of electronic benefit transfer (EBT) across the nation took less than a decade. Part of the welfare reform legislation passed in 1996 required states to implement EBT by 2002. But many states were already moving in that direction. By the summer of 2004, California became the last state to make the transition to electronic benefit transfer cards. As a result, the federal government was planning to phase out food stamps altogether and rename the program. All over the country paper food stamps were replaced with electronic benefits transfer debit cards based on personal identification numbers, and in many states the debit cards contained other such benefits programs as the Women, Infants and Children Program.

Deterring fraud. For liberals, the application of reinvented government to the welfare system had certain advantages that increased access to the system for the needy and provided them with the security and dignity of an electronic benefits transfer card. (Food stamps were frequently stolen because they could be used as cash, and the card looked like a common credit card, thus saving recipients the humiliation that came with counting out food stamps at the check-out counter.) For conservatives and others troubled by high levels of fraud in a system designed to help only the neediest, the application of reinvented government to welfare had the advantage of allowing governments to become more adept at the detection of errors and fraud.

In the late 1970s four counties in Wisconsin experimented with the creation of a single form for welfare services. Not only was the caseworker's time on each case reduced substantially, but payment errors were cut in half.[44] In the early 1980s, New Jersey began conducting a quarterly match of Social Security numbers of welfare recipients with private and public payrolls—an efficient way to determine whether or not people on welfare rolls were actually employed. In two years the cost savings amounted to more than $45 million, which was more than twice what had been estimated and seven times the cost of setting up the program.[45] By the mid-1990s some states and localities were using biometrics to deter fraud in their welfare programs. By fingerprinting individuals, Los Angeles County was able to deny benefits to people attempting to receive duplicate benefits. In only three years this process saved the county $14 million.[46] In programs such as welfare, where liberals feel that there is never enough money to go around and where conservatives are continually suspicious that people are gaming the system, the enhancements to program integrity made possible by reinvented government have been central to the transformation of the system.

Waivers. Many government programs are designed with a provision allowing certain rules to be waived, if necessary. This was the case with the old welfare system, Aid to Dependent Children. But traditional bureaucracies that seek to perpetuate the status quo often discourage applications for waivers—wrapping them up in red tape and generally signaling states and localities, "Don't bother." This changed in the early 1990s. Having decided to pursue health care reform legislation before pursuing welfare reform legislation, the Clinton administration decided that, as a matter of policy, it would encourage states to submit applications for waivers from certain welfare rules. Waivers were granted that allowed states to place a time limit on welfare and that permitted changes in employment programs. Other waivers increased the earnings disregard, changed the family cap, and changed the work requirement time limit. All in all the flood of waiver requests grew substantially as the administration let it be known that it was open to flexibility in the old programs, as Table 5.1 indicates. Waivers allowed for substantial reform in the system even before passage of the reform legislation in 1996.

The importance of waivers as a method of promoting innovation in the public sector cannot be underestimated. If waivers are encouraged,

Table 5.1   Number of Major AFDC Waivers Approved

1992	1993	1994	1995	1996
12	10	15	42	37

Source: "Table B. Approval and Implementation Dates of Major AFCD Waivers Policies, 1992–1996," Department of Health and Human Services, Washington, DC, at aspe.hhs.gov/hsp/waiver-policies99Table_B.PDF.

not discouraged, by the leadership of public-sector organizations, they can serve as powerful indicators of what needs to be changed. In the case of welfare reform, waivers representing the key aspects of a reformed program that encouraged work were granted and implemented prior to national legislation. But in some cases where legislation is not politically feasible waivers also end up being a back-door to reform.

For example, for quite some time it has been clear to students of public administration that federal civil service law (Title V) was in need of a fundamental overhaul. The law permitted a small number of experiments to take place with Office of Personnel Management (OPM) approval. Yet in spite of many successful experiments over the years, such as the navy's experiment at China Lake, California, the experiments remained just experiments. There was little movement toward systematic reform. In the later years of the Clinton administration and the first term of the Bush administration, this pattern was reversed. The Bush's first director of the OPM, Kay Coles James, made it a policy to encourage agencies to utilize the exceptions in Title V. As a result, a large number of federal employees were exempted from the law. Like the welfare system before actual passage of the welfare-reform bill, the federal civil service system has been reformed through a series of incremental, agency-level actions and department-level legislation without passage of a government-wide civil service law.

Table 5.2 summarizes some of the ways the tools of reinvented government have been used to deal with the problems of welfare. Note that reinvented government works best when applied to the eligibility portion of the welfare system, the piece of the system that can be most easily routinized and that needs to be kept under public-sector control. When it comes to welfare clients' transition to work, the reinvented-government strategy that applies is the decision to allow for waivers to government rules. When it comes to prevention and sustaining independence from welfare, two goals that are highly personal and least subject to routinization, there are few clear-cut reinvented-government strategies available.

Table 5.2   Using Reinvented Government to Reform the Welfare System

	Eligibility	Transition to Work	Prevention and Sustaining Independence
Reinvented Government	Reengineer the eligibility process	Grant waivers to states	
	Use electronic benefits transfers		
	Use technology to reduce fraud		

Applying Reinventing Government to the Problem of Homeland Security I

Incremental steps—prevention.   Reinvented government refers to nonincremental, systemic change in the way a government bureaucracy does business. But before we move to how reinvented government applies to the problem of homeland security, we should pause for a moment and consider the fact that incremental steps do not grab headlines but they can be very important.

Some examples of incremental steps include, for instance, Ash Carter's suggestion that in order to prevent potentially disastrous acts of nuclear terrorism we should extend the highly successful and well-thought-out Nunn-Lugar program to Pakistan.[47] This involves an incremental change to an existing program designed to prevent the acquisition and or development of nuclear weapons by terrorists or rogue states. With the discovery of documents on how to make an atom bomb in an Al Qaeda safe house in Kabul, the need for enhancing this program cannot be overlooked.[48] It can be done quickly and does not involve the creation of a new infrastructure, although, as with many ideas in this category, it would most likely entail extra appropriations.

The September 11 tragedies have also focused new attention on the role of money in promoting terror. In October 2001 the Bush administration announced the creation of a beefed-up team to identify and track money being funneled to terrorists. This team will be in the Treasury Department, under the Customs Service, and will expand an already existing team devoted to other financial crimes. As a result of the decades-long war against drugs, the government has in place the expertise for tracking money flows. The expansion of this capacity is a critical but incremental step in the war on terrorism.[49]

Incremental steps—protection. Incremental steps can also be taken to fulfill the mission of protecting the homeland. The first step in protecting our borders from unwanted individuals is the US State Department's consular services. In the fall of 2001, the head of the Bureau of Consular Affairs, Mary Ryan, told a Senate committee that "consular affairs in American embassies and consulates could have stopped some of the terrorists from entering the country if agencies such as the CIA and FBI shared more information with the State Department."[50] A relatively inexpensive, incremental step would be to immediately grant consular officials access to international crime and terrorist databases. Since September 11, the State Department has bolstered its technology to allow consular offices updated "lookout" lists of potential terrorists. It has built a new database called TIPOFF and is in the process of integrating it with terrorist watch lists at the Department of Homeland Security.

Another example of an incremental step would be to deputize state and local officials so that they can arrest illegal aliens, a process now reserved only for federal officers. Senator Kay Bailey Hutchison has introduced legislation that would allow state and local law enforcement to detain and/or arrest and prosecute illegal aliens.[51] The contribution to fighting terror would be immediate and obviously important, although pro-immigrant groups have important and serious concerns about the expansion of policy power into this realm.

In an effort to involve state and local law enforcement more directly, Governor Ridge announced yet another new warning system in response to criticism that the government's warnings on terrorism were inadequate guides to proper action by local police.

Incremental steps can be quite simple and involve very little formal government at all. In an op-ed, Graham Allison suggested that the government and the airlines enlist average passengers in the war against terrorists, instructing them in what to look for and what to do if a terrorist should get on the plane. The model he cites is the safety procedure card that the FAA requires to be placed in every passenger seat pocket.[52] Making everyone more aware and more observant is bound to save lives, especially against something as difficult to detect as terrorism.

Incremental steps—response. Finally, in the response category, the government can require all medium-sized to large US cities to invest in the "all-hazard" approach to emergency response.[53] Because New York City is such a potent symbol and because it had experienced an earlier and potentially devastating terrorist attack on the World Trade Center in 1993, Mayor Rudoph Giuliani had invested in this approach. This involves preparing "first responders—fire fighters, police officers,

EMTs, and other medical personnel first on the scene—to respond to terrorism the same way they'd respond to other disasters, such as floods, hurricanes, toxic spills, plane crashes, and fires."[54] Since the federal government has many ways of forcing states and localities to do what it wants, an effective, if unpopular, method is to tie a goal—in this case emergency preparedness—to some source of federal funding (highways are always popular). A more popular approach is to appropriate money to help the state or locality achieve its goal.

And, a simple but critical action in the realm of response is to increase the amount of drugs available for the civilian population in case of a bioterrorism attack. The first step was begun in the fall of 2002, when vaccinations against smallpox were made available to first responders and the military. Like many incremental changes, this involves new money but money that would be well spent.

The actions summarized in Table 5.3 are incremental in nature because they build on existing law and/or add to existing programs. They are important steps in adapting existing government to new challenges, but they are only the beginning of the challenge.

Table 5.3   Incremental Changes to Existing Government in Light of Homeland-Defense Mission (Examples)

	Prevention	Protection	Response
Incremental Change	Extend Nunn-Lugar to Pakistan Improve means for tracking formal and informal money flows	Provide consular officers abroad access to criminal and terrorist databases Deputize local law enforcement officers so that they can arrest criminal aliens Create an improved warning system for state and local law enforcement Issue guidelines on airline passengers' security responsibilities	Require all medium-sized to large US cities to invest in the "all-hazard" approach to emergency response Increase the pharmaceutical stockpile for civilian use in case of biological-terrorism attacks Vaccinate first responders

Applying Reinventing Government
to the Problem of Homeland Security II

Government reforms in this category are more fundamental and thus more difficult than incremental reforms. They often involve changing the entire orientation of an organization—beginning with its legal context and moving on to the culture in which it operates. Many of the ideas that fall into this category existed before the attacks of September 11 made homeland defense a front-page topic but the absence of a crisis meant that the political will to make such broad-ranging changes was often missing.

Reforming the intelligence community. When the Cold War ended, it became clear that US intelligence had to be rethought and reorganized. As John E. McLaughlin, then deputy director (and later acting director) of the CIA pointed out, the days are gone when the CIA could employ a "canned goods analyst," someone whose entire job was to understand the food-processing industry of the Soviet Union.[55] Well before September 11, the CIA had downsized the Soviet office within the Directorate of Intelligence and had moved considerable resources to a new office, the Office of Transnational Issues, which dealt with the cross-border nature of many emerging threats.

But in a prescient book, predating the September 11 terrorist attacks by a full year, Bruce D. Berkowitz and Allan E. Goodman create a prescription for the post–Cold War intelligence world whose reforms are much more fundamental and far-reaching than the mere moving of resources from one part of the organization to the other. "The intelligence community is a classic bureaucracy, characterized by centralized planning, routinized operations, and a hierarchical chain of command. All of these features leave the intelligence organization ill suited for the Information Age."[56] The bureaucratic organization of the intelligence community worked well when the enemy it tracked, the Soviet Union, was also a bureaucracy and one that in spite of its secrecy moved in glacial and often predictable ways. But to keep up with the new threats, not based in established states, such as terrorism and the enormous changes in capacity resulting from the information revolution, Berkowitz and Goodman propose a radical "reinvention" (my term, not theirs) of the CIA.

The changes that would follow from their analysis are certainly not incremental. For instance, they challenge the need for secrecy in the gathering of intelligence as oddly out of step with the information age (which the intelligence community itself helped create). They also challenge the culture that emerges from secrecy, a culture that reinforces compartmentalization and isolates analysts from each other and from the customers of their intelligence—policymakers.

A second criticism of the intelligence agencies focuses on the tendency to rely on "sigint" (signals intelligence from, for instance, satellite-based eavesdropping) at the expense of "humint" (human intelligence, or good old-fashioned spying). According to former CIA operatives such as Robert Baer, beginning in the late 1980s, the CIA failed to replace the Middle East experts who were leaving the agency. By the end of the 1990s, we had very few or even no operatives capable of penetrating the terrorist movements that had become so dangerous.[57]

In addition, during the 1990s it came to light that a paid informant had been involved in the murder of two people, one an American, and so the CIA director issued a directive that came to be known as the "scrub" order. According to some, this review of recruits, issued with the best of intentions, came to have a chilling effect on the spy business—one that, in conjunction with the shortage of Arabic-language speakers, further impeded our ability to find out what was going on in the world.[58]

It is not at all clear that any of the intelligence failures, evident to many before September 11, 2001, would have prevented the attacks. In hearings before Congress, former CIA officer Milt Bearden pointed out that no one else in the world saw the attacks coming and that infiltrating terrorist cells where everyone is related to everyone else is an inherently difficult task.[59] But previous intelligence failures, such as not predicting nuclear testing in India in 1998 and the demoralizing Aldrich Ames case, were warnings that the intelligence community had not succeeded as well as it needed to in rethinking its routines after the Cold War.

Just as important as reinvention at the CIA is the need for reinvention at the FBI, and reinvention of the relationship between the two agencies. The separation of intelligence between the FBI and the CIA was the result of the excesses of the Hoover-era FBI when files were kept routinely on political dissidents and peaceful protest groups. And the antagonism between the two agencies dates all the way back to World War II when the FBI and the CIA's predecessor, the Office of Strategic Services (OSS), fought over jurisdictional issues.[60] Yet in the aftermath of 9/11 it became clear that terrorism did not fall neatly into the bureaucratic and jurisdictional lines of either the CIA or the FBI, and that changes needed to be made if the government was to be effective in preventing future such acts.

Most of the conversation about the future of the FBI revolves around changing the culture of the organization from one that was focused on seeking indictments and convictions of criminals, *after* the fact, to an organization that could prevent criminal activity of the terrorist kind *before* the fact.[61] Of the government changes that are most difficult, transforming the culture of an organization ranks at the very top. Reinvention enthusiasts, however, often overlook the fact that in this nation's system, culture stems from law and that changing law is the first and often most important step. An important first step came shortly after September 11 with passage of the USA Patriot Act of 2001, which made it easier for the FBI and the CIA to share more sensitive information with each other.

But legal reform is only the beginning of what must be an ongoing effort to transform two very different and sometimes hostile agencies into a coherent and effective preventive force. In the past, the two agencies were quite competent and cooperative when the source of the threat was known well enough that information collected overseas could be neatly passed from a foreign agency to domestic law enforcement. But prevention requires a much more fundamental assessment of foreign and domestic intelligence. It requires ongoing and systematic analysis of both foreign and domestic bits of data and an organization that can weave them into a coherent picture. This is a systemic problem, illustrated by what happened and what did not in the government prior to September 11. It is succinctly summarized by two authors of a best-selling book about 9/11 and it has been reinforced by subsequent government panels that looked into the pre-9/11 problems.

> We found in almost every case that the cops, agents and spies who followed their instincts were on the right trail. But we found a recurring pattern. Over and over again the investigators were waved off the right trail. The reasons ranged from risk-averse bosses to bureaucratic structures that seemed designed to ensure that the left hand would never know what the right hand was doing.[62]

How should the government reinvent itself to undertake the transformation of agencies like FBI and CIA? Each one has to add the terrorism problem on top of older, more traditional problems. The FBI still needs to catch mobsters and drug kingpins; the CIA still needs to monitor conventional military movements in states like North Korea, and it still needs to track a much less sharply defined problem.

Experience with reinvented government shows that the combination of performance measures and attention to the incentive structures faced by front-line personnel is often a starting point for major improvements in an organization's performance. In New York City the combination of crime statistics and accountability from the front line forced a fundamental change—Comstat—in the crime-fighting paradigm. Instead of being rewarded for catching criminals, an activity that takes place after a crime has been committed, the police began to be rewarded for preventing crime in the first place.

Comstat in New York City effectively changed the incentive structure of the front lines from prosecution to prevention. By focusing on the incentive structures faced by individual FBI agents, the agency should be able to create incentives for prevention and keep the traditional imperative for prosecution from interfering

In addition, CIA and FBI agents need to take a page from the military reforms of the 1980s and engage in another aspect of reinvented government—cross-training. CIA officers are now routinely stationed at many of the FBI's terrorism task force centers across the country, and FBI agents are increasingly stationed abroad. Experts in the collection and analysis of intelligence regularly train FBI agents: to transform the FBI into a more effective counterterrorist organization, those experts established a new career path for FBI special agents. This path gives all agents experience in intelligence collection, analysis, and dissemination and makes intelligence officer certification a prerequisite for advancement.[63]

But, as the military found, these efforts work only if they are formalized. Cross-agency service—all too long resisted by those who wanted to move up in the bureaucracy—must now become a staple for those who would become leaders.

This means, too, that the walls within the CIA must be bridged. Isolating counterterrorism in a unit, no matter how big or well funded, apart from the established international geographical units, will not be as effective as forcing a regular interchange among those with regional and those with terrorist expertise. In the private sector, companies use the rotation of employees and matrix management to break down boundaries between divisions and specialized entities. The rotation is at once a strategy and a culture as stated by an early work on the topic titled "Matrix Management; Not a Structure, a Frame of Mind." In it Christopher Bartlett and Sumantra Ghoshal caution that, "Keeping a company strategically agile while still coordinating its activities across divisions, even continents, means eliminating parochialism, improving communication and weaving the decision making process into the company's social fabric."[64]

The concept of matrix management is one of those private-sector techniques that can be especially important to reinvented government. In the intelligence community, for instance, it may not be practical or advisable to make people rotate jobs. After all, the community needs serious technical knowledge and ability in things like the interpretation of satellite imagery and the construction of small nuclear devices. And it needs deep cultural, social, and language expertise in various regions, countries, and ethnic conflicts. But what the United States learned the hard way in the first decade of really trying to deal with transnational threats is that "transnational issues require combinations of regional and functional expertise."[65] In other words, just because a new set of issues is "transnational" does not mean that national and regional knowledge is irrelevant. In fact, "terrorism has a base—when you separate it out from its regional base you lose something."[66]

The systematic strategic rotation of analysts with functional expertise into units with people who have expertise in regions and nations may be one way to prevent the kinds of mistakes that happened in Iraq when technical knowledge was not related to its political and social context. An internal review of the problems leading up to the incorrect intelligence in Iraq concludes that offices focus narrowly on functional and technical issues and that intelligence needs to be integrated into data produced by regional or country analysis units.[67] The challenge before the intelligence community is to retain and reward expertise while creating a culture that communicates across divisional lines.

Finally, the episodic nature of terrorism is likely to mean that attention to it will wax and wane. Thus one option is to create an entity whose sole mission is to look for puzzle pieces from Buffalo to Baghdad. One of the suggestions coming from a Harvard University "executive session" on catastrophic terrorism (held three years before the September 11 tragedy) bears repeating today. The idea was to create an FBI national terrorism intelligence center. As a separate organization this entity would

> combine the proactive intelligence gathering approach of the national security agencies, which are not legally constrained in deciding when they may investigate a possible crime, with the investigative resources of law enforcement agencies. We must have an entity that can utilize our formidable but disparate national security and law enforcement resources to analyze transnational problems. This combination should be permitted, consistent with public trust, only in a National Center that has no powers of arrest and prosecution and that establishes a certain distance from the traditional defense and intelligence agencies. The Center would also be subject to oversight from existing institutions, like the federal judiciary, the President's Foreign Intelligence Advisory Board and the select intelligence committees of the Congress.[68]

This concept is somewhat different from that of the CIA's Terrorist Threat Integration Center. There are indications that this entity has contributed to some important steps in the war on terror, but the 9/11 Commission's recommendation for the creation of a national counterrorism center indicates that an even stronger and more independent integrative function is needed.

Protecting the borders. Obviously we need to increase the nation's protection right at its borders. To do this, the government has finally acted on an idea that has been around for many years, creating a border patrol agency. The concept of such an agency is at the heart of the new Department of Homeland Security, for most of the money and the people in that department deal in one way or another with the borders.

Protection of the borders should begin outside the United States, with the particular agency charged with allowing people, first off in their places of origin, into the country. Before foreigners can get into the United States they need a US visa. Overworked consular officers, generally young diplomats trained in diplomacy, not police work, are given the responsibility of deciding who gets to come to the United States and who doesn't. In recent years consular officers have, of course, been under extreme stress. Not only has the number of people wanting to come to the United States increased dramatically, but for many years Congress starved the entire State Department (including the consular section) of funds.

According to former State Department official T. Wayne Merry, "visa work is a low prestige poor relation to the conduct of diplomacy and always low in budget priorities. The professional consular corps is often highly competent but is badly overworked, under financed and so few in number as to staff only supervisory positions."[69]

So the first step in creating a new agency is to upgrade the consular affairs section and turn it into an agency that has the intelligence and the resources to weed out dangerous people before they even get to the United States. It should be moved out of the State Department and formed into a group of those who combine the unique blend of diplomatic, language, and detective skills needed to detect dangerous people before they leave their country. The legislation creating a Department of Homeland Security (DHS) took a very timid step in this direction by giving the new department control over the issuance and denial of visas but keeping the actual agency in the State Department—an awkward compromise that will probably not work in the long run.

The second step is to tackle the enormous problem of securing our borders against terrorists and weapons of terror while maintaining our participation in a global economy. Historically we separate protection of the borders into two bureaucracies. One agency, the Customs Service, is supposed to protect us against bad things; the other, the Immigration and Naturalization Service (INS), is supposed to protect us against bad people. This bureaucratic bifurcation has never worked very well. The two agencies exist side by side at the borders and ports of entry, but that has not prevented them from engaging in bitter feuds. The extent of this dysfunction at the borders was brought home on June 29, 1995, when the system suffered a meltdown in Miami. As passengers waited in the summer heat at Miami International Airport to get through Customs and INS checkpoints, fist fights broke out. Flights had to circle the airport or to be diverted, since there was no way additional passengers could get into the airport. With the growth in international trade and travel, the pressures on Customs and INS only increased.

Thus, long before 9/11 there were calls for the creation of a separate border patrol agency that would combine the services and improve the functions of the US government at the nation's borders. But this idea was consistently opposed by concerned agencies themselves, their congressional sponsors (and whichever attorney general and treasury secretary happened to be in office at the time). One attempt to combine the three main agencies—Customs, INS, and Coast Guard—had been proposed by President Herbert Hoover in 1930 and 1932 and almost enacted into law. In the intervening years the idea kept coming up.[70] In 1993 the National Performance Review floated a proposal to create a border patrol agency. It created such intense divisions in the Clinton administration and opposition from the attorney general and treasury secretary that it was watered down to read "Improve Border Management" in the final National Performance Review report.[71]

But what was not politically possible before September 11 became possible after. Protection of the borders is now a core element in homeland defense—and the task is enormous. For instance, Stephen E. Flynn has written persuasively of "terrorist needles in a transportation haystack." "In 2000 alone, 489 million people, 127 million passenger vehicles, 11.6 million maritime containers, 11.5 million trucks, 2.2 million railcars, 829,000 planes, and 211,000 vessels passed through U.S. border inspection systems."[72]

Problems of a similar scale exist because of the human factor. The sheer amount of international travel has increased dramatically in recent times, and all agencies charged with handling the problem have been plagued by problems that go back years. Globalization of the economy and cheaper air travel, among other things, have meant a huge increase in the number of foreigners coming to the United States: from fiscal 1981 to 1998 the annual number of visitors admitted with visas nearly tripled to 30 million.[73] The INS has been unusually slow to adapt, leading two members of Congress to call it "the most dysfunctional agency in all of government," a sentiment echoed by everyone who has ever had anything to do with the agency.

Unlike the Bureau of Consular Affairs, the problems of the INS cannot be blamed on lack of money, since Congress has consistently increased the service's funding in recent years. In spite of this, on September 11, the INS was still processing applications by hand, having inexplicably failed to acquire the electronic systems that would help the process. When it bought new systems, such as that to counter smuggling, the INS failed to train employees to use them. The service has been chronically unable to keep track of its weapons or property, as various inspector general reports have shown over the years.

The INS's failures are not new. During the Iranian hostage crisis in 1979, the service was able to track down only 9,000 of the 50,000 Iranian students in the United States. In 1993, the INS had no idea that Jordanian Eyad Ismoil had violated his student visa until he drove a bomb-laden truck into the World Trade Center.

It is well known that the INS does not do a very good job of getting people out of the country who have overstayed their visas. The INS itself estimates that 40 percent of all illegal immigrants come to the United States with visas but do not leave when their visas expire.[74] Of the hundreds of people who have been detained as suspects since the 9/11 attacks most are being held on immigration charges. The agency reported recently that a computer network to track foreign students in the country was still being tested and would not be ready for another year—even though Congress had ordered it six years ago![75]

In its 2002 budget the Bush administration proposed splitting the INS into two parts, which was a good idea and long overdue. In April 2002, the House passed a bill to accomplish this and the attorney general, echoing President Clinton's famous pledge to "end welfare as we know it," vowed to "end the INS as we know it."[76] The naturalization part of the service, which makes legal immigrants into citizens, would be kept in the Justice Department and transformed into an agency dealing with those wanting to become US citizens. But the Border Patrol part of INS was eventually moved to the new Department of Homeland Security, where one hopes it will be able to overcome a well-deserved reputation for incompetence. Persistent failure at the INS was ignored when the consequences involved only illegal Mexican gardeners and housekeepers. But the need to reinvent the INS was one of the most powerful arguments in favor of creating a new Department of Homeland Security, since the INS has been notoriously resistant to incremental changes.

The reorganization of agencies at the border is the one part of the new DHS that makes the most organizational sense. In commenting on the proposed new department, many private-sector gurus, burned by large-scale mergers that did not work out, have warned against large-scale organizations in analyses that sound like my own critique of the bureaucratic instinct in Chapter 4. Although their warnings should be heeded, the situation at our borders is one that is very unlikely to be found in the private sector. For one thing, the front-line workers of those agencies working the borders are already in one place, so reorganization offers substantial opportunities for organizational synergies. Think of the current border situation as an assembly line for cars where one set of workers puts on the doors, a second installs windshields, and a third paints the finished product. Each set of workers reported to different managers in separate organizations with separate personnel structures, rules, and money. Such an assembly line would not work very well and neither did the pre-DHS border setup before the department's establishment. The border patrol portion of the DHS actually changed the situation on the ground and on the front line—something that all too many reorganizations fail to do.

As we have seen, however, this new department cannot be allowed to replicate the dysfunctions of the old departments. It must be created as a reinvented public-sector organization. For instance, as currently configured, Customs and the INS are ill equipped to stop terrorism without also stopping commerce. That won't do. Right now, for example, the system has a hard time analyzing risk and using technology; so at this early stage in the history of the department we have the worst of both worlds. Legitimate travelers and businesses are inconvenienced and subject to increased costs, but terrorists are not found.

Accomplishing goals of organization reform and border protection will require enormous investments in data and in a wide range of technologies. The new system will have to figure out how to determine risk, and the average citizen will have to be willing to spend something for convenience.

During the Clinton administration a plan emerged to create an international trade data system, but the plan was killed by a combination of vested interests. For instance, one of the reasons for the plan's demise was how much more open to examination the vast array of goods crossing US borders would be.[77]

Finally, there is no tougher issue in US politics than racial profiling. And yet, when terrorism originates in and is sponsored by people from certain physically identifiable groups, it is absurd to be forced to ignore national origin or ethnicity in protection of the borders. There needs to be a process whereby racial profiling is allowed as *one of many* variables in a preventive strategy—for instance, where intelligence and other tips indicate that doing so would contribute to the protection of the public. This is part and parcel of moving law enforcement from acting after the fact to becoming part of protecting Americans by preempting terrorist acts.

Another very touchy issue is posse comitatus—a law passed in the wake of the Civil War and Reconstruction that limits the military's role in domestic affairs and serves to keep the military out of police work. However, there are many terrorist attack scenarios in which the military would be the only organization capable of aiding in a response. For instance, a simultaneous outbreak of some very dangerous and easily transmitted disease such as smallpox or the Ebola virus in US cities could require immediate prohibitions on travel. It is likely that this would quickly strain the capacity of local and state law enforcements, and soldiers would need to be brought in to enforce a quarantine.

President George W. Bush's own response plan for catastrophic attacks anticipated situations in which first responders would not be able to respond to them. In such situations, the secretary of the Department of Homeland Security is authorized to declare a catastrophic emergency and engage the US military. Unfortunately this plan was issued only days before a huge natural disaster, Hurricane Katrina, not a terrorist attack, hit the United States. Unfortunately for the people of New Orleans, too few leaders in Washington understood their own plan and consequently spent precious days debating their legal authority before finally calling up the military inside the homeland. For many people that intervention was simply too late. In most catastrophic scenarios time is of the essence. Therefore, as in the case of racial profiling, it behooves the government to reevaluate the laws and practices of the various agencies involved and create new protocols for a new world.

Table 5.4 summarizes some examples of reinvented government in pursuit of homeland security. Unlike the incremental steps listed above, these actions involve far-reaching change in public-sector bureaucracies, and they sometimes borrow modern management strategies from the private sector in order to improve performance. But these changes take place within the public sector and deal with aspects of the problem, such as intelligence gathering and border protection, that are, in the judgment of most people, core governmental activities. The next chapter explores a broader set of actors in the implementation of policy.

Conclusion

The twentieth-century response to problems was to create new bureaucracies. But in the twenty-first century greater attention must be given to the more difficult work of transforming old organizations into new, flexible organizations. Fundamentally, this means moving from rule-driven organizations to those that are performance driven, conveying the changes to the organizations' front-line workers and creating cultures in which information flows horizontally between organizations.

Using homeland security as an example, the reforms most likely to deal with the problem do not happen at the level at which budgets are written and grand policy is made. Instead they involve thinking hard about such topics as the culture of secrecy in, for instance, the CIA and whether or not that culture impedes intelligence in an information age. It involves changing the incentive structure of the FBI so that performance at the level of individual agents is measured in preventive terms as well as in cases successfully prosecuted. It involves using the notion of productivity through successful action at the borders to maximize security while continuing to promote trade and commerce. And it involves a greater degree of cross-agency coordination than ever before.

Table 5.4   Using Reinvented Government to Achieve Homeland Defense Missions (Examples)

	Prevention	Protection	Response
Reinvented government	Reinvent the intelligence agencies	Consolidate and reinvent the agencies that work at the borders	Establish guidelines for circumstances under which posse comitatus restrictions should not prevent military deployment
	Reinvent the traditional relationship between foreign intelligence and domestic law enforcement	Add consular affairs to the new Department of Homeland Security	
	Create an entity responsible for analyzing foreign and domestic intelligence to look for terrorism	Develop new technologies for speedier movement of goods and people across borders	
		Resurrect the international trade data systems plan	
		Establish guidelines for circumstances under which the use of racial profiling may be justified	

In the area of welfare reform, reinvention involved using information technology to streamline eligibility processes into the program, thus improving the productivity, accuracy, and integrity of the program. Welfare reform, as we will see in the next chapter, has been characterized by a decision to end the monopoly of the state in terms of the delivery of services. The public sector has de facto limited its role to the eligibility and compliance functions most suited to a public sector organization, and it has turned to other organizations to complete the rest of the policy mandates.

Homeland security and welfare reform are two examples of how, in the next century, a relatively small portion of government functions will be totally controlled by public-sector organizations, reinvented or not. The challenges of problems in the twenty-first century mean that policymakers need to move outside the public sector and direct new and more complex forms of governance.

Notes

1. See, for instance, B. Guy Peters and John Pierre, "Governance without Government? Rethinking Public Administration," *Journal of Public Administration Research and Theory* (April 1998).

2. Quoted in Peter Evans, "The Eclipse of the State? Reflections on Stateness in an Era of Globalization," *World Politics* (October 1997): 65.

3. Robert O. Keohane and Joseph S. Nye Jr., "Introduction," *Governance in a Globalizing World,* eds. Joseph S. Nye and John D. Donahue (Washington, DC: Brookings Institution Press, 2000).

4. H. George Frederickson, "The Repositioning of American Public Administration," The John Gaus Lecture, *PS Magazine*, December 1999, 705.

5. James P. Pinkerton, *What Comes Next: The End of Big Government and the New Paradigm Ahead* (New York: Hyperion, 1995).

6. Ibid., 62.

7. Ibid., 63.

8. Herbert Kaufman, *Are Government Systems Immortal?* (Washington, DC: Brookings Institution Press, 1976).

9. Pinkerton, *What Comes Next,* 64.

10. Ibid., 65.

11. Ibid., 66.

12. President Clinton and Prime Minister Blair used the term "third way" to refer to a political platform that served to move the Democratic Party and the Labour Party away from their "statist" pasts.

13. Elaine Ciulla Kamarck, "The Globalization of Public Administration Reform," in *Governance in a Globalizing World* (Washington, DC: Brookings Institution, 2000).

14. As various scholars attempt to categorize what is going on in the post-bureaucratic state they have used a variety of terms. For instance, what I describe here as reinvented government, others have described as "market-type

bureaucracies." See Mark Considine and Jenny M. Lewis, "Governance at Ground Level: The Frontline Bureaucrat in the Age of Markets and Networks," *Public Administration Review* 59, 6 (November/December 1999).

15. Statement of J. Christopher Mihm, acting associate director, Federal Management and Workforce Issues, *Performance Based Organizations: Lessons from the British Next Steps Initiative*, Washington, D.C: US General Accounting Office, GAO/T-GGD-97-151 (July 8, 1997).

16. Ibid., 6.

17. Elaine Ciulla Kamarck, "Globalization and Public Administration Reform," *Governance in a Globalizing World.*

18. Salvatore Schiavo-Campo, "Government Employment and Pay: The Global and Regional Evidence," *Public Administration and Development* 18 (1998): 457–478.

19. Ibid., 466.

20. This is the lesson that emerges from David Osborne's *The Price of Government*, which details the remarkable stability, over time, in the tax burden that voters are willing to tolerate.

21. "Benchmarking E-Government: A Global Perspective: Assessing the Progress of the UN Member States" (New York: United Nations Division for Public Economics and Public Administration and American Society of Public Administration, May 2002).

22. See "The UK Government Approach to Public Service Reform—A Discussion Paper," (London, Whitehall, Public Service Reform Team Strategy Unit, June 2006), 66.

23. Thanks to John Kamensky, IBM Center for the Business of Government, Washington, DC, for these insights.

24. See Laurence E. Lynn Jr., "Requiring Bureaucracies to Perform: What Have We Learned from the U.S. Government Performance and Results Act?" (Paper prepared for presentation to the Ninth International Research Meeting of the Journal Politiques et Management Publique, Aix-en-Provence, May 28–29, 1998).

25. John Buntin, "Assertive Policing, Plummeting Crime: The NYPD Takes on Crime in New York City" (John F. Kennedy School of Government Case Study 1530, July 11, 1990).

26. Swati Desai and Michael Wiseman, "Inside the Help Factory: Public Assistance Process, Outcome and Opportunity in New York City" (Paper presented at the Association for Public Policy and Management Research Conference, November 2002). Thanks to my student Andrew R. Feldman for making me aware of this paper.

27. "Life after Civil Service Reform: The Texas, Georgia, and Florida Experiences" (IBM Endowment for the Business of Government, Washington, DC, October 2002).

28. Harvey Simon and Malcolm Sparrow, "Regulatory Reform at OSHA" (John F. Kennedy School of Government Case Study 1371).

29. See Charles Rossotti, *Many Unhapy Returns: One Man's Quest to Turn Around the Most Unpopular Organization in America* (Boston: Harvard Business School Press, 2005).

30. Prime Minister's Public Service Conference, Queen Elizabeth II Conference Center, London, June, 6, 2006.

31. John Rudy and Ivan Eland, "Special Operations Military Training and

Its Dangers" (Foreign policy briefing, Cato Institute, Washington, DC, June 22, 1999), 5.

32. Graham Allison and Peter Szanton, *Remaking Foreign Policy: The Organizational Connection* (New York: Basic Books, 1976), 121.

33. For a history of these reforms, see James R. Locher III, *Victory on the Potomac: The Goldwater-Nichols Act Unifies the Pentagon* (College Station: Texas A & M Press, 2002).

34. Linda de Leon and Robert B. Denhardt, "The Political Theory of Reinvention," *Public Administration Review* (March/April 2000): 92. They comment that "the 'shadow' side of the entrepreneur is characterized by a narrow focus, an unwillingness to follow rules."

35. Considine and Lewis, "Governance at Ground Level," 475.

36. Jeffrey D. Kubik, "Fiscal Federalism and Welfare Policy: The Role of States in the Growth of Child SSI," *National Tax Journal* 56, 1 (March 2003): 61.

37. Karl Kronebusch and Brian Elbel, "Enrolling Children in Public Insurance: SCHIP, Medicaid, and State Implementation," *Journal of Health Politics, Policy and Law* 29, 3 (June 2004).

38. Phil Bodrick, "Rethinking Welfare Management," *Government Executive* 27, 9 (September 1995): 16A.

39. Ibid.

40. Robert Peck, "Integrated Systems Improve Welfare Delivery," *The American City and County* 17, 1 (January 2002): 10.

41. William Welsh, "States Back Off Large Welfare System Projects," *Washington Technology*, November 16, 2000.

42. Loren Bell et al., "Re-engineering the Welfare System," Economic Research Service, FANRR-17, US Department of Agriculture, July 2002.

43. Norma M. Riccucci et al., "The Implementation of Welfare Reform Policy: The Role of Public Managers in Front-Line Practices," *Public Administration Review* 64, 4 (July/August 2004).

44. Marguerite Zientara, "Single Form, Net Cut Payment Errors in Half," *Computerworld* 12, 23 (June 5, 1978): 27.

45. Valerie Englander and Fred Englander, "The Cost Effectiveness of Computer-Based Welfare Fraud Detection in New Jersey," *Public Productivity Review* 9, 2/3 (Summer/Fall 1985): 271.

46. Government Accounting Office, "Electronic Benefits Transfer—Use of Biometrics to Deter Fraud in the Nationwide EBT Program," Washington, DC: US Government Accounting Office GAO/OSI-95-20 (September 29, 1995).

47. Ash Carter, "The Architecture of Government in the Face of Terrorism," *International Security* 26, 3 (Winter 2001/02): 5–23.

48. "We Must Act as if He Has the Bomb," *Washington Post,* November 18, 2001, Outlook section.

49. "Agents to Track Money," *Washington Post,* October 26, 2001.

50. See http://www.govexec.com/dailyfed/1001/101201b2.htm.

51. "Bill Would Let Police Detain, Arrest Illegal Immigrants," *Daily Texan,* February 10, 2006.

52. Graham T. Allison, "Preventing Terrorism in the Air: A How-to Guide for Nervous Airline Passengers," *Chicago Tribune,* November 20, 2001, section 1.

53. Lory Hough, "Terrorism in America," (John F. Kennedy School of Government, *KSG Bulletin,* Autumn 2001, 17–23).

54. Ibid., 21.

55. Speech by John E. McLaughlin, April 2, 2001, Special to washingtonpost.com/ac2/wp-dyn/A17769-2001mar30?language=printer.

56. Bruce D. Berkowitz and Allan E. Goodman, *Best Truth: Intelligence in the Information Age* (New Haven and London: Yale University Press, 2000), 67.

57. Robert Baer, *See No Evil: The True Story of a Ground Soldier in the CIA's War on Terrorism* (New York: Crown Publishers, 2002), 95.

58. Seymour M. Hersh, "What Went Wrong: The CIA and the Failure of American Intelligence," *New Yorker,* March 18, 2002, 34–42.

59. Steve Hirsch, "CIA Performance Disputed as Congress Plans Hearings," *Global Security Newswire,* April 1, 2002.

60. For a history of this stormy relationship, see Mark Riebling, *Wedge* (New York: Alfred A. Knopf, 1994).

61. "Ashcroft Plan Would Recast Justice Department in a War Mode," *New York Times,* November 9, 2001.

62. John Miller et al., *The Cell* (New York: Hyperion, 2002), 4.

63. Congressional testimony of FBI Director Robert S. Mueller III before the Senate Committee on Intelligence, February 16, 2005.

64. Christopher A. Bartlett and Sumantra Ghoshal, *Harvard Business Review*, 68, no. 4 (July 1990): 138–145.

65. Interview with a former CIA official, spring 2005.

66. Ibid.

67. Private communication with the author, spring 2005.

68. Ashton B. Carter, John M. Deutsch, and Phillip D. Zelikow, "Catastrophic Terrorism: Elements of a National Policy" (Report of the Visions of Governance for the 21st Century Project, Cambridge, MA, Harvard University, 1998). See www.ksg.harvard.edu/visions.

69. "How Visas Can Perpetrate Terror," *Washington Post,* September 28, 2001.

70. Frederick M. Kaiser, "Reorganization Proposals for U.S. Border Management Agencies" (Washington, DC: Congressional Research Service, July 22, 1999).

71. Vice President Al Gore, *Creating a Government That Works Better and Costs Less: Report of the National Performance Review* (Washington, DC: Government Printing Office, September 7, 1993), 151.

72. Stephen E. Flynn, "The Unguarded Homeland: A Study in Malign Neglect," in *How Did This Happen? Terrorism and the New War,* eds. James F. Hoge Jr. and Gideon Rose (New York: Public Affairs, 2001), 187.

73. "Tougher Enforcement by INS Urged," *Washington Post,* September 18, 2001.

74. Ibid.

75. "Efforts to Track Foreign Students are Said to Lag," *New York Times,* January 28, 2002.

76. CNN, April 25, 2002.

77. Jane Fountain, *The Virtual State* (Washington, DC: Brookings Institution Press, 2002) for a description of this program and the politics that killed it.

6

Government by Network

IN RECENT YEARS, the term "network" has become very popular and has been used to describe a wide variety of complex social relationships. When applied to government, the term has come to have at least four separate meanings:

- policy formulation networks
- nonstate governance networks
- state-to-state or federalist networks
- government-created networks

Often "networked government" is used to describe the constellation of organizations, (public, private, and semi-public) that influence a policy world—in other words, a policy network. This use of the term "networked" is not very new and is similar to what an earlier generation of political scientists might have termed "the iron triangle" of bureaucrats, congressional staff, and interest groups.[1]

"Network" has also come to describe organizations in the private sector that take on governance responsibilities within a certain portion of the market. For instance, Timothy Sinclair has written about the bond-rating agencies of the private sector as "embedded knowledge networks." These entities derive their authority not from any government sanction but from "epistemic authority."[2] One of the most important examples of a private organization that contains no government but still exercises a governmental function is the Internet Corporation for Assigned Names and Numbers (ICANN), established by the US Commerce Department to assign domain names to Internet sites. It was built on the very broad participatory ethos of the early cybernetics pioneers who insisted that the Internet could be governed without government.[3]

Network has also been used to describe emerging relationships between states. As the economy has become global, the need for global governance measures has increased. But international bureaucracies have proved even less attractive to states than their internal, domestic bureaucracies. The bureaucracies of the UN and the emerging European Union (EU) bureaucracy in Brussels are rife with "bugs" in their operating systems and burdened with suspicion about their degree of accountability. For this reason world government is a "nonstarter" with all but the most sanguine futurists.

Instead, as Anne Marie Slaughter and others have stated, the response to the need for international governance has been for subunits of national governments to develop relationships in which both law and administrative processes are harmonized, thus allowing for governance in the place of actual government.[4] In one study, John Peterson and Laurence O'Toole use the term network to apply to the complex, mutually adaptive behavior of subunits of states in the EU, a process that is often slow and opaque but also solves an important supranational governance problem.[5] Wolfgang H. Reinicke writes that "a more promising strategy [than global government] differentiates governance and government."[6] Joseph Nye points out that understanding the new world of governance involves thinking of a "three dimensional chess board" where private, public, and third-sector actors interact with supranational, national, and subnational actors.[7]

In the United States a long tradition of federalism means that individual states have been participants in an important policy and implementation network. This network has allowed for the diffusion of innovations from state to state, through governors' conferences and the promulgation of such tools as model statutes. The diffusion of innovation among states has allowed them to live up to their billing as the "laboratories of democracy."[8]

The first three ways in which "network" is used are primarily descriptive of naturally occurring processes in complex, modern, globalized societies. While they are not especially new, the computer revolution has given us new metaphors to use in describing these processes. And social scientists are finding these organic modes of governance ripe fields for study—as they well should.

But for our purposes in defining new, postbureaucratic modes of policy implementation, the fourth use of network is the most relevant. That is why instead of referring to "networked government" I will use the term "government *by* network." In government by network the state makes a conscious decision to implement policy by creating a network of nongovernmental organizations through its power to contract, fund, or coerce. In government by network, the state itself decides to create, activate, or empower a network for the purpose of implementing a policy. Thus the network is a self-conscious creation of a policymaker or a group of policymakers rather than a naturally occurring part of the greater society.[9]

To some, this mode of policy implementation diminishes the role of government. H. Brinton Milward and Keith G. Provan have dubbed this form of government the "hollow state."

> [T]he hollow state refers to any joint production situation where a governmental agency relies on others (firms, nonprofits, or other government agencies) to jointly deliver public services.... The main difference between the hollow state and direct government provision of services lies in the presence of a bureaucratic mechanism.[10]

They go on to make the point that in spite of the prevalence of this form of government, we know relatively little about how to manage networks.[11]

Government by network is certainly not new, but there is some indication that it has become more prevalent. In one study of nonprofit organizations, Steven Smith and Michael Lipsky found that in the last half of the twentieth century government funding of nonprofit social-service organizations increased substantially in the sample of organizations studied.[12] In the 1950s government funding of nonprofit agencies was minimal, but by the end of the decade the situation was very different. In a brief description of thirteen social-service agencies in Massachusetts, the authors show that in 1960 only two of the agencies received government support, and public dollars constituted only a small percentage of their revenue. By 1970, eight of the thirteen agencies were receiving government funding, and for three the amount was substantial. By 1980 every agency was receiving government funding, and in all but three agencies it constituted over 50 percent of their total revenues.[13]

The extent to which government business is conducted through a network of nongovernment organizations was brought home to most Americans during the federal government's shutdown of 1995–1996. All sorts of organizations found themselves starved by the sudden absence of federal money.[14] In *Governing by Network: The New Shape of Government*, Stephen Goldsmith and William D. Eggers cite data from the federal government showing that between 1990 and 2001 contracting jumped by 24 percent and data from the Government Contracting Institute showing that government contracts to private firms rose 65 percent between 1996 and 2001 for state and local governments. They cite increased contracting in all government areas, from schools to prison management to military operations, and conclude that the public sector is being transformed from a "service provider to a service facilitator."[15]

Across the Atlantic the British government created a new Office of the Third Sector as part of the Cabinet Office with the express purpose of encouraging charities and other third-sector organizations to "contribute to the diversity of services on offer." The Blair government has decided that, as a matter of policy, it wants to increase the involvement of private-sector management in the public sector. To support its choice the government points to the history of "contestability" in the management of the prison service begun in 1991. After fifteen years of experience it was found that "the cost per prisoner of privately managed prisons is 10–15% lower than comparable publicly managed prisons."[16] Examples from around the world were cited, such as Australia's use of contractors in employment services in the form of the national Job Network, a reform responsible for a fall in the cost of labor-market programs.[17] These examples are meant to support greater "contestability" in implementing policy.

One explanation for the increased use of networks and the increased attention to them is that, until recently, government by network has been largely an unconscious choice on the part of policymakers. They have sought to create networks out of a desire to avoid traditional bureaucracies. Hence, networks have become popular implementation choices for what they are *not* (i.e., bureaucracy) as opposed to what they are. In government by network, the traditional control mechanisms of the bureaucracy become less important (and less frustrating) to the person seeking performance in government. As Lester M. Salamon points out: "Under these circumstances, the traditional concerns of public agencies—their personnel systems, budgetary procedures, organizational structures and institutional dynamics—have become far less central to program success."[18]

Characteristics of Government by Network

In government by network the bureaucracy is replaced by a wide variety of other kinds of institutions, almost all of which have better reputations (and sometimes better performance) than government itself. In government by network, the government stops trying to do things itself; instead it funds other organizations that do the actual work the government wants done. Most government organizations do contract out some of their work some of the time, but the key to government by network is that a substantial portion of the work is contracted out.

The variety of organizations that have been part of government by network is immense: churches, research laboratories, nonprofit organizations, for-profit organizations, and universities have all been called upon to perform the work of the government. Some look at the emergence of this form as a "hollowing out" of the state, but it pays to remember that the sum total of all this activity by different kinds of organizations is still something that the state wants done. When the state opts to create a network it is because the work wanted would not occur to the same extent without the resources and direction of the state.

Government by network has two major attractions: (1) it is not bureaucratic, (2) it has the potential to be flexible and to innovate—characteristics in short supply in traditional bureaucracies. In fact government by network has been used in the past when a government valued innovation so much that it was willing to give up a certain degree of control.

As bureaucratic government has failed or has developed bugs in one policy area after another, policymakers have looked to implement policy through networks instead. Because government by network tends to be a default position for policymakers, the characteristics of government by network have rarely been articulated to the same degree as in the reinventing-government movement.

But as we will see when we look at some recent examples from very different policy areas—welfare to work, intelligence collection and analysis and homeland security—it is possible to discern some implicit and explicit characteristics of government by network. When the government chooses to create a network it generally does so in areas where the public-policy outcome tends to be amorphous and impervious to routinization. In addition, it seeks to involve a wide variety of nonpublic organizations in the work as a means of promoting innovation. Because a government-run network ideally includes a wide variety of actors, the state chooses to value innovation over conformity even though, as we saw in Chapter 3, the loss of transparency can cause political problems or performance problems. Finally, when the state chooses to create a network it *should* seek to learn from the overall operation of the network. On this last point "should" is used quite consciously. Given that government by network is fairly new, it is clear that the government does not always capture the learning from the network that it should.

As modern governments look to create networks to implement policy they create dilemmas for the participants in those networks. Often, the participants in government by network end up being private-sector groups that started out criticizing government policy. The decision to join a government network changes the relationship of many groups with the government. According to the leader of one nonprofit group,

"Once civil society gets engaged and gets a contract—your ability to criticize is diminished as the government contributes 50% of your budget."[19] Nonetheless, modern governments are increasingly drawing "third-sector" groups into their implementation structures.

Applying Government by
Network to Transition to Work

The year 1996 saw the end of a welfare system that had been almost universally regarded as a failure. As we saw in Chapter 4, the old welfare system was characterized by its bureaucratic attention to detail, especially its insistence that applicants meet all the rules and that social workers fill out all the paperwork properly. In typical bureaucratic fashion, the imperative from the federal government that state governments minimize errors in eligibility meant that the people in the system focused on eligibility at the expense of assistance.[20] Not surprisingly, the welfare system came to be seen as a program that maintained people in poverty instead of getting them out of poverty.

An early attempt at welfare reform, the Family Support Act of 1998, created the JOBS program with the laudable intent of getting people off the rolls and into jobs. But this program managed to be strangled by bureaucracy as well. Evelyn Brodkin describes how the bureaucratic culture of rules caused states to retain their focus on eligibility determination. This culture conflicted with the need for flexibility inherent in dealing with human problems. She described Chicago's JOBS program as follows:

> Department executives often were confounded by caseworker discretion and the apparent imperviousness of caseworkers to management exhortations to demonstrate "compassion," abide by processing rules, and promote employment as a client goal. (In part, management's problems derived from contradictions inherent in those objectives; e.g., between adherence to standardized rules and responsiveness to client needs.)[21]

Like so many other systems, the welfare system as it existed at the end of the twentieth century was a closed system, run by the bureaucratic imperative and organizationally impervious to the needs of welfare mothers. It was a failed system. In 1988, David Ellwood, in his book *Poor Support,* made the liberal case for fundamental change in the welfare system and advocated replacing it with a system "that encourages and rewards work and responsibility."[22] Ellwood showed Democratic politicians, especially the future presidential candidate, Bill Clinton, how to replace the widely reviled system with one that promised better outcomes for the people who became part of it.

Eight years later a new law, the Personal Responsibility and Work Opportunity Reconciliation Act (PRWORA), was enacted which replaced the old AFDC system with a new work-based system. From a decade of research policymakers knew certain things. They knew that welfare recipients needed day care and extended medical care. So the new law provided for more day-care subsidies and for Medicaid past the time when welfare mothers went back to work. But the law also provided that a substantial amount of money be given to states to pay for welfare-to-work programs in order to get at the very difficult problem of treating and preventing long-term welfare dependence. This the government did not know how to do. In fact, years of experience with welfare programs had taught policymakers that the government bureaucracies administering payments had been, by and large, pretty awful at actually helping welfare mothers get and hold jobs.

By the 1990s, policymakers on both the left and the right acknowledged that the welfare system had a serious performance deficit and so they opted to give the states an unprecedented amount of freedom to create welfare-to-work networks. Policymakers knew that they wanted, in a very general sense, to promote economic independence among former welfare recipients, especially the long-term welfare recipients the previous system had failed. But they did not know the best way to accomplish this. In fact, there probably was no one best way that would work for different individuals; getting formerly dependent welfare mothers to work was a task that was impossible to routinize—thus the network concept made sense. The law provided that these networks could consist of not-for-profit organizations (a traditional piece of the social-service network), for-profit corporations, and religious organizations (the last a new addition to the federally financed welfare world).

Government did not try to do this work. In a dramatic abdication of control, government at the state and federal level as much as admitted that government bureaucracies were not suited to this sort of work: the work of getting welfare mothers to work should be given to whoever could argue persuasively to the government that they could accomplish the goal.

To be sure, contracting out of various human services had been increasing before passage of the 1996 welfare reform act. In fact, a Council of State Governments 1993 study reported that almost 80 percent of state social-service departments surveyed had expanded their use of private services in the previous five years. In addition, a report to Congress in 1997 found that state and local privatization of social services had continued to expand and that the percentage of program budgets paid to contractors had increased since 1990, as had the number and variety of programs contracted out.[23]

Thus the 1996 law made explicit what had been implicit. It had an immediate effect on the private sector. Take, for example, Lockheed Martin, a giant American corporation that almost single-handedly exemplifies the military-industrial complex. Imagine how surprised people were when, in 1996, Lockheed Martin IMS (a subdivision of the company) announced that it was going into the welfare-to-work business. From supersonic airplanes to welfare mothers? The corporation was simply using its years of experience in government contracting to get into the latest and one of the biggest government sectors ever—social services. For the anticorporate do-gooders of the old left, this was a jarring but inevitable development when government creates a network in place of a bureaucracy.

Another actor in the network, one of Lockheed Martin's competitors for this business, Maximus, tells potential investors in its advertisements that social services administration is a potential $21 billion market.[24] And Peter Cove, founder of America Works, one of the oldest for-profit welfare companies in existence, urges local governments to set tough standards for their contracts, knowing that his company will then have a greater advantage over competitors.[25]

Not only did the government invite the private sector into the welfare-to-work realm to compete with the nonprofit sector (which had been a staple of social services), it invited in the religious world as well. A segment of the law called the "charitable choice" provision allowed governments to contract directly with churches and other religious organizations for the provision of services. Under previous contracting provisions, the government could only contract with religious organizations that had spun off a tax-exempt organization and promised to do no proselytizing in the course of administering the social services. But under the new law religious doctrine was permitted (with some constraints) in the delivery of welfare-to-work services. To those concerned about the First Amendment and the separation of church and state, this was an ominous development. But it was also an indication of how far the government wanted to go in encouraging diversity and innovation in this particular network.

The welfare-to-work network embodied all the characteristics of government by network. It was a conscious policy decision designed to meet a goal, which was to get former welfare recipients to be independent, a policy impossible to routinize. It permitted the involvement of a wide array of different organizations and different approaches for the purpose of maximizing innovation. But it is still difficult to know what actually worked. We know that the number of people on the welfare rolls has dropped and that according to a Department of Health and Human Services (HHS) study, "these are the longest caseload declines in the history of U.S. Public Assistance Programs."[26] But we do not really know why the overall caseloads have dropped and, more important for the purposes of this book, we do not really know how well the welfare-to-work network itself is working.

Of all the characteristics of government by network, ensuring learning by the network may be the most difficult. While evaluations done on the macro level tell us some important things (e.g., employment-based welfare-to-work programs tend to help the most disadvantaged recipients more than education-based programs), the accrued learning needs to make it down to the state or county official who contracts with the array of providers allowed in the law. That is the level at which a network really begins to learn from itself. As we saw in Chapter 3, if government by network is mismanaged, it may take on all the problems of traditional government.

Applying Government by Network to Preventing Welfare Dependence and to Sustaining Independence

Effective enforcement of child support payments is essential to keeping people (almost always women) off welfare and is thus another key element of any successful policy aimed at reducing welfare dependence. Poor women who have never been married are less likely to have child-support agreements and to actually receive any more money than their better-off sisters. In fact mothers on AFDC were almost half as likely as women not on AFDC to have a child-support agreement.[27] Thus getting child support orders and collecting on them is critical to keeping women off welfare. Part of the welfare reform legislation of 1996 was a requirement for states to begin integrating various databases in order to make it easier to find deadbeat fathers and maybe garnish their wages. By 2004, all but a handful of states had been certified by HHS as having created an automated child-support enforcement system in keeping with the specifications of the 1996 bill.

This was a major information technology reinvention but it has been augmented by a trend among states to contract out the hardest to collect to private collection agencies. In so doing government is making use of the expertise in an existing private-sector industry, bill collection, and is expanding the market for those industries to include the public sector. As in many instances where the government decides to do its work through a network of private-sector providers, this move has not been without controversy. But effective child-support payment collection is an important part of keeping welfare rolls down, as found in a recent study. [28]

A decade ago private firms specializing in tracking down deadbeat parents hardly existed, but now there are approximately thirty-eight companies in the business.[29] Mostly they advertise to women on television and on the Internet, and have run into controversy for taking a hefty portion of the unpaid child support they collect (sometimes as much as 34 percent).[30] But the 1996 welfare reform legislation created a new set of incentives for states to improve their child-support payments collection performance. As states sought to reduce their welfare rolls and their Medicaid costs, they also sought to increase the amount of child support actually paid.

Between 1990 and 1994 alone the child-support caseload in the United States increased by 45 percent, from 12.8 million to 18.6 million.[31] States suddenly found themselves without the personnel to keep up with the cases. In some states individual caseworkers had up to 2,500 cases.[32] So a number of states decided to contract out their cases in which payments were hard to collect, allotting the contracts on a contingency-fee basis. A ready and willing set of bidders was found among private-sector specialists in bill collection, who could often track down a deadbeat father in a fraction of the time it had taken the old bureaucracy. A 1996 Government Accounting Office (GAO) study found that even after the fees paid to the collection agencies, states were experiencing a net gain in child-support revenues.[33]

In this field of collection, as in other areas where a state decides to create or enable a network, innovation is the most important reason. For instance, there is a Georgia couple that runs World Collections, a business originally founded to track down debtors for lenders such as Wells Fargo. The two have been helping the state of Georgia track down deadbeat parents. They do not get paid unless they succeed, but they bring enough expertise to the job so they can often conduct a search in only thirty minutes. They enjoy significant advantages over the state employees involved in the same tasks, who have individual caseloads as large as 1,000 and who have only one Internet source—in contrast to the five sources regularly used by World Collections. The state pays World Collections $99 per search, which is less than the $340 private clients pay but more than the $25 that it costs the state to do a search.[34]

As with welfare-to-work programs, learning may be one of the biggest challenges for those in government who decide to create or enable a network. But one example from Maryland illustrates how com-

Table 6.1   Using Government by Network to Reduce Welfare Dependence

	Eligibility	Transition to Work	Preventing Welfare Dependence and Sustaining Independence
Government by network		Work provisions of the 1996 welfare-reform act allow a large number of actors to perform the service	Use private/for-profit contractors to collect child-support payments from delinquent parents

petition from government by network has created significant learning and change in the public sector. Lockheed Martin was hired to collect child support in two Maryland counties in 1996 as part of a plan to see if the entire program should be taken away from the state and turned over to private contractors. But Lockheed Martin fell short of its first-year goal, while public employees in another Maryland county, where employees had been freed of some traditional bureaucratic restrictions, increased their collections by 13 percent.[35] This story has been repeated in many jurisdictions. Years ago, the city of Indianapolis began to outsource garbage collection only to have its unionized employees win back contracts after examining their own work procedures. If there is a mechanism for learning from government by network it can become a powerful tool for creating reinvented public-sector organizations.

Table 6.1 summarizes some of the ways that government by network can be used to reduce welfare dependence. Note that there are really no good examples of government by network in the area of establishing eligibility, which, as most jurisdictions have agreed, should remain firmly in the public sector. But other pieces of the problem, especially those in need of innovation, seem to have benefited from government by network.

Government by Network Applied to Homeland Security

The welfare-to-work provisions of the 1996 welfare-reform law are but the latest and most expansive in a long history of using government by network in the world of social services, where the problems are as complex as the individuals social-service systems seek to help. But government by network is not applicable to the social-service realm only. The diversity and capacity for innovation inherent in a network is likely to make government by network a staple of law enforcement and the fight against terrorism as well. Even before the tragedy at the World Trade Center it was clear to many that the bureaucracy was a major impediment in the fight against international crime and terrorism. Pieces of these puzzles crossed a number of agencies—the INS, the CIA, the FBI, and the Customs Service—to name a few. Each of these agencies grew up in a time when the world was more or less neatly divided between internal and external threats. The amorphous nature of terrorism, organized international crime, and such new crimes as cyberterrorism means that the closed worlds of intelligence agencies and law enforcement agencies will have to change.

Tipped off to an attack or in the aftermath of an attack, cooperation between government agencies and even between the government and the private sector tends to be effective. But in the case of catastrophic terrorism there is no substitute for preventing the attack. The prevention challenge is especially difficult, for in the era of terrorism not sponsored by any state it is an exercise in trying to know the unknowable. In the new world of terrorism, the bureaucracy of the old intelligence community lacks both flexibility and imagination.

The CIA has been trying to cope with this new world. In an unclassified report called "The Ecology of Warning," the agency declared the following:

> We need new frameworks or lenses for every aspect of the warning function.... Traditionally, warning has focused on military threats where the range of possible outcomes is relatively limited.... The warning community now extends well beyond the [intelligence community], military and the national command structure to include the local police, public health authorities and the financial community among others.[36]

In that same report, the CIA lists some steps that can be taken today. It recommends encouraging partnerships with new domestic and foreign players, such as local police forces and nongovernment organizations. It calls for identifying roadblocks to cooperation and dialogue across organizations. It challenges one of the longest held parts of the intelligence community's culture by recommending knowledge sharing and ways of sharing information without specific source or method attribution. In essence, the agency is trying to figure out a path from the intelligence bureaucracy of the Cold War era to the more flexible and imaginative structure needed to meet the terrorist threat. The structure the CIA is outlining sounds very much like a structure in which nongovernment organizations would become linked in a network whose purpose is the implementation of government goals.

In a book published a full year before the September 11 attacks two intelligence experts, Bruce D. Berkowitz and Allan E. Goodman, predicted the kind of reforms that are now being discussed in the intelligence community. In *Best Truth: Intelligence in the Information Age,* they take on one of the sacred cows of intelligence work: the famous "need to know" and its concomitant culture of secrecy. This culture results in extreme compartmentalization, one of the biggest problems with traditional bureaucracy and one of the "bugs" in the system that makes traditional bureaucracy incompatible with the information age. "The procedures and technologies of the Information Revolution—open architectures, public databases, and the ability to form networks with almost anyone, anywhere—are all defeated by secrecy."[37]

Like the welfare-to-work networks of the recent past, which were designed to meet the goal of self-sufficiency, the intelligence networks of what is hoped to be the near future will need to meet the goal of national security. Just as it is impossible to routinize methods for getting welfare mothers to work, there are no routines for monitoring emerging threats that do not have a country, a military, or even, sometimes, a name. Bureaucracy only works when there is at least a chance for standardization and routinization. In the absence of the ability to establish routines, it makes sense for the government to involve a wide variety of nonpublic organizations in a network designed to meet its needs.

Government by Network
Applied to National Identification

Compared with other countries, the United States has a very decentralized government. Indeed most of American history has involved some form of discussion about federalism: the proper relationship between national government, state, and local governments—and deep suspicion of centralized government. Homeland defense starts up that conversation again. The sheer number of jurisdictions, laws, regulations, and operating protocols that make up the US federal system are designed to defy control by any one entity—which is exactly what Americans have always wanted. So how does one improve homeland security in a system that is intentionally, indeed passionately, decentralized? Here is where the concept of government by network, applied to the vast system of government jurisdictions of this nation, comes in handy.

Take the issue of national identification, a problem critical to the prevention of terrorism. Among the many holes in the country's domestic defense is a very lax system of acquiring identification cards, namely drivers' licenses. In fact, as Shane Ham and Robert Atkinson point out, most American teenagers possess fake IDs in order to drink alcohol. The practice is so common as to be almost a rite of passage.[38] One solution to the problem has been to issue a national identification card, which, of course, would require a new federal bureaucracy to be layered on top of existing state bureaucracies. It also invokes images of "big brother" and would be bound to be as unpopular today as in the past. It is typical of bureaucratic responses to problems so common in the preceding century.

In contrast to the creation of an entirely new identification system, Ham and Atkinson proposed the creation of a public-sector network (my terms, not theirs). The proposal would modernize the current system by having Congress issue guidelines and provide appropriations for the standardization of drivers' licenses. They proposed that Congress require states to issue "smart ID cards" that contain "a standardized hologram and digitally encoded biometric data specific to each holder."[39] In addition, they recommend that Congress set higher standards for documentation before issuing such identification cards and that Congress provide funds for linking state motor vehicle departments' databases. "This would virtually eliminate the practice of ID poaching, and if tied in with a smart visa proposal, would prevent foreign visitors from obtaining driver's licenses and then hiding out in the United States after the visas expire."[40]

This way of thinking about the problem of national identification was eventually built into the legislation that emerged from the report of the 9/11 Commission. It prevailed, in spite of fears that it was a "back door" national identity card, because it built on the federalist system by using national power and federal money to form a network of state motor vehicle departments. This network will cost more than the present states' systems but not as much as the creation of a brand new bureaucracy, and it will not engender the inevitable opposition to accretion of centralized powers in a country which is historically a decentralized state. Finally, it will most surely increase security and help prevent terrorists from getting the documentation they need to operate in the United States.

Forging a network like the one proposed by Ham and Atkinson has further interrelated advantages. Tighter security around drivers' licenses will probably reduce the number of accidents due to teenagers' drunk driving and make the crime of identity theft more difficult. Since terrorism is apt to be a sporadic and intermittent threat, when reforms are made that offer other advantages to society that are not related to terrorism, these should be emphasized and promoted so as to secure continued political and budgetary support for the reforms. Thus the existing reforms will be kept from withering on the vine—a particular problem in a society where memories are short and news cycles and political attention are even shorter.

Government by Network Applied to Local, State, and National Coordination

Government by network is even more important in the next two categories of homeland security policy, protection and response. Since 9/11, long-simmering anger among local law enforcement organizations toward the FBI for its traditional reluctance to share information has come to the surface.[41] Shortly after the attack, we learned that the FBI did not share information about suspected terrorists with Michael Chitwood, chief of police of Portland, Maine, the point of origin for the Logan Airport–bound hijackers. And in early 2002, New York City officials were particularly upset by two episodes: they were not told about the anthrax-bearing letters or about a nuclear threat to the city. This led the two US senators from New York to sponsor a bill that would permit, but not require, the FBI to share information about potential terrorist attacks with state and local police forces. In April 2002, then Attorney General Ashcroft released a plan ordering the development of protocols for sharing relevant terrorism-related information among sections of the Justice Department, especially the FBI, and state and local law enforcement agencies.

Thousands of words have been devoted to the importance of creating this kind of public-sector network, but it is clear that the information flow leaves a lot to be desired. Three years after Ashcroft's directive, the FBI led Massachusetts authorities to believe that two Iraqis and four Chinese scientists were about to unleash a nuclear attack on Boston. The "rumor" quickly made it into the press, creating a high level of readiness and causing Governor Mitt Romney to race back to Massachusetts and miss President Bush's second inaugural ceremony. The leak published in the press left Washington feeling that it was justified in not trusting locals; locals thought Washington made them jump through hoops for nothing. The much-heralded era of cooperation between federal intelligence organizations and state and local government was clearly not yet in place.

Government by Network
Applied to Emergency Response

Like intelligence sharing, response to terrorist acts (or any catastrophic events), involves all levels of government because the first people on the scene ("first responders") are always local police, fire, and medical personnel. But one of the biggest changes in the twenty-first century is the realization that public health is part of national security. In the case of a bioterrorism attack, the very definition of "first responders" would have to change. First responders in a bioterrorism attack would very likely be nurses, doctors, and laboratory technicians. In terrorism-related budgets prior to September 11, the bulk of the money went to law enforcement and defense, with public health a poor sister. Beginning with the anthrax attack in the fall of 2001, and moving through the SARS crisis and the threat of an avian influenza pandemic, we have realized that we do not know very much about health as a national security threat. As the confusion around the anthrax attacks in the fall of 2001 proved, the US government is ill equipped to respond to such attacks. In a role-playing episode at the end of the 1990s, the DOD declared the right to seize command during a bioterrorism attack in spite of its limited experience in public health matters.[42] Constitutional issues aside, the DOD has many capabilities, but expertise in disease and contagion are not among them.

Thus, in preparing for the future and for the need to respond to totally new and unexpected forms of terror, the United States needs to build a series of response networks that involve all levels of government and to practice reactions to scenarios that can only be imagined. Identifying the spread of a very rare disease such as smallpox on a national level, tracking its progress, acquiring and moving stocks of vaccine, communicating with the public, placing affected people in quarantine, shutting down travel—the list of steps to be taken and the confusion that would result from missed steps are a nightmare in and of themselves. The only way to prepare is the way the military does: with practice, practice, and more practice. But the number of different entities involved is huge, and each one has other, important, day-to-day responsibilities to the public. These entities must be rehearsed and molded into a network that, when needed, can operate as one.

How to do that? Right before the September 11 attacks, Army Lt. Col. Terrence Kelly published an article on homeland defense in which he suggested borrowing a concept from the military: a commander in chief (CINC) for homeland defense.[43] The last major reorganization of the US military dealt with the traditional divisions (and rivalries) between the services and the need to make these historically separate bureaucracies into a coherent force in battle. As a result, the regional CINC command structure in the DOD gives one person the power and authority to plan for and then, if necessary, command, the assets of the different parts of the military. Kelly was suggesting the CINC concept for a Homeland Defense Agency, but the CINC option has even more utility when applied to the need for coherent response.

FEMA is the logical place to locate all emergency responses. But, as Hurricane Katrina showed, the agency's capacities have been sorely degraded by its inclusion in the Department of Homeland Security (DHS). There are many people who believe that FEMA should be restored to its independent status, and a bill was introduced into the Senate following the hurricane that would do just that.

FEMA should not only have its independence restored, with its director having cabinet rank, it should be given more resources and the formal authority to act as CINC in the preparation and coordination of federal, state, and local governments to respond to all kinds of terrorist events. Given the complexity of the task at hand, an independent and reinvigorated FEMA is the most likely candidate to force other federal agencies, such as the Centers for Disease Control, and state and local governments into an effective response network.

Even before FEMA was melded into the DHS, the Senate was reluctant to make clear the lines of authority in this critical area, insisting that FEMA share first-response and training authority and grant making with the Department of Justice Office of Domestic Preparedness. Once FEMA was made part of DHS it lost its grant-making authority altogether and was, as became evident during Hurricane Katrina, forced to the sidelines.

As the simulation known as "Dark Winter" proved, a smallpox attack on the United States can cause massive confusion and death.[44] In that exercise, the sticky issue of federalism arose. Former Senator Sam Nunn, who played the president of the United States, said at one point, "We're going to have absolute chaos if we start having war between the federal government and the state government."[45]

The sooner a CINC-like authority is vested in FEMA the better. The creation of a first-rate response network will also fulfill an important criterion of homeland defense reform mentioned above. Improvement in the coordination of responses to terrorism will improve the coordination of responses to all sorts of catastrophes, whether or not the result of terroristic acts. An independent and empowered FEMA will again attract first-rate talent, but it needs a clearer mandate both inside and outside the federal government. The hapless director of FEMA during Hurricane

Table 6.2   Using Public-Sector Networks to Achieve Homeland Security Mission (Examples)

	Prevention	Protection	Response
Government by network (public)	Modernize the state identification (drivers' licenses) systems	Create a network between the FBI and state and local law enforcement that would permit sharing of information on terrorism threats	Adapt the CINC model with FEMA as the lead agency in charge of training, gaming, and command

Katrina, Michael Brown, was widely criticized for his lack of relevant experience. His manifest unfitness for the job led some to blame the political patronage system. And yet, James Lee Witt, the widely admired FEMA director during the Clinton administration, was also a political appointee and much closer to the president than George Bush's "Brownie." The issue is experience and authority, which can come in political appointees as well as in career personnel.

Table 6.2 summarizes some of the ways public-sector networks can accomplish parts of the homeland security mission.

Government by Public- and Private-Sector Networks Applied to Intelligence and Response Missions of Homeland Security

As we have seen, government by network is an important tool for building greater security in a fragmented, federalist governmental system. But it is an equally important tool for involving the private sector in homeland defense. For instance, the private sector has pioneered the use of "data mining," the process of analyzing large databases to construct information, usually about sales or about market trends, that is not immediately evident from raw data alone. This is an expensive and carefully guarded process, but it could potentially allow the government to find clues important to its mission in preventing terrorism.

An early example of the use of data mining in terrorism comes from the former West Germany in the 1970s. A law enforcement officer named Horst Herold helped create a major breakthrough against the domestic terrorists of the Red Army Faction. By mining private-sector databases such as travel companies, utilities, and even pension funds he was able to create prescient profiles of where the terrorists would be and how they would behave. Herold turned the West German Federal Crime Office into an "unparalleled crime-fighting machine."[46]

His efforts were, however, not without controversy, since significant proprietary issues and privacy issues arose as a result of his crime-fighting innovations. The West German system he created was eventually dismantled. Thus there is an important caveat to the use of data mining: when a government elects to establish a network involving the private sector to help do public business it needs to protect privacy and property. These issues need to be carefully negotiated and implementation carefully monitored. Government by network survives ultimately on trust that the public's privacy will be protected and that market information and other intellectual property of the business sector will be protected.

That trust was severely and dramatically absent in the Pentagon's attempt to use a form of data mining in the Total Information Awareness Project run by retired Admiral John Poindexter. That project would have scanned commercial databases of health, financial, and travel companies here and abroad to look for terrorists. But the choice of Poindexter to lead the project (he had been convicted of lying to Congress during the Iran-Contra controversy but subsequently cleared on a technicality) only increased the distrust. Internet and privacy activists took on Poindexter personally—revealing where he lived and other personal information. Civil libertarians on the left and right banded together, and by January 2003 the Senate had voted to curb the project.[47]

Much less ambitious attempts to draw the private sector into a security network have also failed. Prior to 9/11 the Clinton administration had in place a system for identifying suspicious airline travelers, the Computer Assisted Passenger Profiling System. This system served to identify many of the eventual 9/11 hijackers, but they were singled out only for extra baggage screening—a function of the government's looking for terrorists who were going to place explosives on planes, not hijackers who intended to commit suicide. In the aftermath of 9/11, the DHS started the development of a much more ambitious system called CAPPS II. As of this writing, CAPPS II has not been deployed. Trials with the system designed to test it were subjected to immediate lawsuits from passengers, and airlines concluded that they simply could not share the information needed unless they had a clear federal requirement to do so.

The difficulty of creating a security network of public and private databases shows just how powerful the old bureaucratic paradigms are. The old security paradigm involved states' bureaucracies spying on other states' bureaucracies to assess military plans and intentions. The new security paradigm involves states attempting to identify threats hidden in the private sector. The only way this can be done is through government by network, but the requisite trust needs to be built first.

How can that happen? One option would be to place administrators of various large private-sector databases under the legal obligation to monitor and report suspicious patterns themselves to the government. This would involve training certain people at, for instance, credit card companies in what to look for and establishing protocols for when it is important to share certain patterns or information with the government. This would allow the private sector to keep its trade secrets and customer information to itself and yet be on the lookout for patterns signaling potentially dangerous activity. It would also allow the government access to those patterns without engaging in "spying" on private citizens.

Finally, it would enable the government to increase its learning about terrorists and their ways. In a world where threats are embedded in the private sector instead of in foreign governments, our government runs the risk of not learning what it needs to learn. Nowhere is this difficulty more evident than in the need to protect the nation's information systems from cybernetic attack. In May 1998, the Clinton administration issued Presidential Decision Directive 63 on critical infrastructure protection, acknowledging that a new source of vulnerability to asymmetric warfare had opened up in the United States as a result of our increasing reliance on cybernetics-based systems to operate every part of our economy. The directive created the National Infrastructure Protection Center in the FBI. The cybernetics security problem, however, has proved to be typical of many twenty-first-century problems, in that solving it involves significant cooperation and regular cooperation from the private sector.

But the private sector has been exceedingly reluctant to cooperate. In a survey conducted by the Computer Security Institute in April 2002, 94 percent of the respondents reported having detected security breaches of their information systems in the preceding twelve months, but only 34 percent reported the intrusions to any law enforcement agency.[48] A 2005 survey from the same group found that "the percentage of organizations reporting computer intrusions to law enforcement has continued its multi-year decline. The key reason cited for not reporting intrusions to law enforcement is the concern for negative publicity."[49] The lack of reporting also stems from fears that the government will not adequately protect the customers or the proprietary information of private companies. Lack of trust is having severe consequences for the ability of law enforcement to protect us from cybernetics-based attacks, and will continue to do so.

When Senator Bob Bennett, a Utah Republican, sponsored the

Critical Infrastructure Information Act of 2001 (later incorporated into the Homeland Security Act), he said that trying to devise a protection plan for the Internet without candid information is like "trying to run a battle, when 85% of the battlefield is blind to you."[50] And Director Robert Mueller of the FBI "implored" industry technology executives to do more reporting of incidents of such crime so that the bureau could do a better job of in protecting the private sector.[51] One of the key provisions of Bennett's legislation was to exempt from the Freedom of Information Act certain information likely to be disclosed in any case of a cybernetics-based attack and an investigation.

For government to do its job, a network has to be created in the private sector that will allow it to learn what it needs to deter, detect, and prosecute crime. As in the case of data mining, the creation of such a network for cybernetic security is fraught with concerns for privacy and for property protection. Nevertheless, earlier generations worked out protocols for wiretaps on telephones that served the country well and that, on the whole, served to protect civil liberties. The new imperative is to develop similar protocols, which will allow the government to use the vast databases of the private sector to protect us from terrorists.

As is the case with so many new problems, the problem of cybernetic security cannot be contained within US borders. Before he left the White House, White House Security Advisor Richard Clarke was pushing for a global system modeled on the successful Y2K-style center set up by the United States to deal with the computer problems anticipated at the turn of the twenty-first century. However, even as officials in Europe and the United States debated the virtues of a new global center for information technology security, others were not so hopeful after the failure of similar efforts by the Group of Eight industrialized countries.[52]

As has been clear throughout this chapter, effective homeland defense will require the development of many new technologies. As our experience in weapons development over many decades has shown, innovation in technology cannot be limited to the public sector. The Soviet Union tried that and lost. William Bonvillian and Kendra Sharp have proposed the creation of another Defense Advanced Research Projects Agency (DARPA) for homeland-security technology.[53] DARPA is best known to the public as the creator of the Internet and is one of, if not *the*, most successful technology development agencies in history. Critical to the success of DARPA is that government used its money and power to enlist all manner of actors from universities and from the private sector in the innovation process. It was once referred to as "75 geniuses connected by a travel agent"—in other words, government by network.[54]

Government by Network
Applied to Emergency Response

As we have seen, government by network plays an important role in prevention and protection. It also has a critical role to play in the response to terrorism. Recent trends in medicine in the United States have resulted in less capacity to deal with a "surge" in demand for serious medical care than ever before.[55] Innovations such as "just-in-time" inventory systems for equipment and drugs, and the increase in outpatient care as drug therapy has replaced surgery and hospitalization for some illnesses, means that this country does not have the infrastructure to deal with mass injuries. The absence of "surge capacity" is serious when contemplating a high number of injuries resulting from a terrorist attack involving explosives. The absence becomes even more dangerous seen in light of the number who would need medical care that could arise from a biological terrorism attack. In such an attack everything from sterile equipment and clothing to isolation wards would become inadequate almost instantly.

It is unrealistic to expect that an overburdened and increasingly expensive private health care system can develop and maintain the capacity to treat massive numbers of victims of something like a big terrorist attack. However, it is not unrealistic to expect that the government could lead the private sector in the development of a plan whereby the location of medical supplies would be known, plans for their delivery formalized, and locations for makeshift hospital beds and isolation wards identified ahead of time. In other words, working with both the private and public health care sector the government could create a network in every major metropolitan area in the United States that would be dedicated to the instant creation of emergency hospitals. In the immediate aftermath of the 9/11 bombing of the World Trade Center, an emergency medical unit was set up in downtown Manhattan and access to that borough was cut off to everyone except medical personnel, who knew they had to come into the city. This had been practiced and planned because Mayor Rudy Giuliani had had some warning stemming from the 1993 World Trade Center attack.

Another important element of response is found in the media. For days after the September 11 attacks, most Americans were glued to their televisions. Especially in the case of a biological attack, the media have a role to play in conveying useful information and preventing panic. Matt Meselsen, an eminent biologist and expert on biological terrorism at Harvard University, pointed out that in thinking about a biological attack we need to start by "thinking small."[56] Creating a list of these "small things" that people could do to prevent the spread of disease and then working with national and local media to educate them on the likely course of an attack could save lives and prevent the panic that is often the goal of terrorists.

The importance of effective communications in responding to a terrorist attack was emphasized by former senator Sam Nunn. In testimony before Congress on the lessons learned from participating in "Dark Winter," he said: "How do you talk to the public in a way that is candid, yet prevents panic—knowing that panic itself can be a weapon of mass destruction? My staff had two responses: 'We don't know,' and 'You're late for your press conference.' I told people in the exercise: 'I would never go before the press with this little information, and Governor Keating—who knows about dealing with disaster, said: 'You have no choice.' And I went, even though I did not have answers for the questions I knew I would face.'"[57] In the case of a biological attack, the president of the United States needs to know what to do, but the public will need to see not only politicians; trained medical personnel who have useful, simple words of advice for a panic-stricken and confused public will be essential.

The Federal government's feeble response to the disaster of Hurricane Katrina pointed out all too clearly what happens when the management of a network fails. All the contracts were in place for dealing with a large-scale disaster (e.g., everything from trailers to ice ready for delivery); however, FEMA officials allowed one unnecessary delay after another in implementation, prolonging the suffering and increasing the losses.

Table 6.3   Using Public- and Private-Sector Networks to Achieve Homeland Security Missions (Examples)

	Prevention	Protection	Response
Government by network (public and private)	Create a network with the private sector that would utilize modern data-mining techniques	Create a network for protection of critical infrastructure Create a small agency based on the DARPA model to innovate in homeland-defense technology	Develop plans for "surge capacity" in the public—and private—health care sectors Create a network of emergency response, medical leaders, and broadcast journalists for cases of biological attacks

Table 6.3 summarizes some of the ways that public- and private-sector networks may be used to achieve homeland-security missions. All the examples used show that the government needs to develop a network in the private sector.

Conclusion

Government by network is a powerful and increasingly commonly used method of dealing with complex modern problems that require constant innovation, from welfare to intelligence to homeland security. Government by network is also being used extensively in other areas of human services and in the environmental area.[58] But the term is used in a wide variety of ways, thus confusing policy formulation networks with the network as a conscious policy implementation choice. Thus seeing the network as a self-conscious alternative to the bureaucracy is another way to understand the network's potential as an alternative method of policy implementation.

Notes

1. See, for instance, Paul Sabatier and Hank Jenkins-Smith, eds., *Policy Change and Learning: An Advocacy Coalition Approach* (Boulder, CO: Westview, 1993).

2. Timothy J. Sinclair, "Reinventing Authority: Embedded Knowledge Networks and the New Global Finance" (Paper presented to the Annual Meeting of the American Political Science Association, August 28–31, 1997).

3. Zoe Baird, "Governing the Internet: Engaging Government, Business and Nonprofits," *Foreign Affairs* (November/December 2002): 15–20.

4. "The Real New World Order," *Foreign Affairs* 76, 5 (September/October 1997).

5. "Networks and Governance in Europe and America: Grasping the Normative Nettle" (Paper prepared for Rethinking Federalism in the EU and the US: The Challenge of Legitimacy, John F. Kennedy School of Government, Harvard University, April 19–21, 1998).

6. Wolfgang H. Reinicke, "Global Public Policy," *Foreign Affairs* 76, 6 (November/December 1997).

7. Joseph S. Nye Jr., *The Paradox of American Power: Why the World's Only Superpower Can't Go It Alone* (New York: Oxford University Press, 2002), 46.

8. See, for instance, David Osborne, *Laboratories of Democracy,* (Boston: Harvard Business School Press, 1990); and John Peterson and Laurence J. O'Toole Jr., "Federal Governance in the United States and the European Union: A Policy Network Perspective," in Kalypso Nicolaidis and Robert Howse, eds., *The Federal Vision: Legitimacy and Levels of Governance in the United States and the European Union* (New York: Oxford University Press, 2001).

9. Stephen Goldsmith and William D. Eggers use the term "governing by network" to describe this self-conscious selection of the network as a policy implementation option. See *Governing by Network: The New Shape of the Public Sector* (Washington, DC: Brookings Institution Press, 2004).

10. H. Brinton Milward and Keith G. Provan, "Governing the Hollow State," *Journal of Public Administration Research and Theory* (April 2000): 362, 363.

11. Ibid., 1.

12. *Nonprofits for Hire: The Welfare State in the Age of Contracting* (Cambridge, MA: Harvard University Press, 1993).

13. Ibid., 236–237.

14. While it seems as if government by network has increased over the past few decades in the social-service area, the overall picture is difficult to assess. One piece of research, based on a comparison of federal law at two points in time (1965–1966, 1993–1994) shows no change in the use of nonstate actors to implement programs. See Thad E. Hall and Laurence J. O'Toole Jr.,"Structures for Policy Implementation: An Analysis of National Legislation, 1965–1966 and 1993–1994," *Administration and Society* 31, 6 (January 2000): 667–686. However, a much more exhaustive analysis is needed, one that includes legislation at the state level. In addition, the selection of the 1965–1966 period, which included passage of much Great Society legislation, could skew the results.

15. Goldsmith and Eggers, *Governing by Network*, 10.

16. *The UK Government's Approach to Public Service Reform: A Discussion Paper* (London: Public Service Reform Team, 2006).

17. Ibid., 51.

18. Lester M. Salamon, "The New Governance and the Tools of Public Action: An Introduction," *The Tools of Government: A Guide to the New Governance*, Lester M. Salamon, ed. (New York: Oxford University Press, 2002), 12.

19. Private conversation with the head of an international NGO, Wilton Park Conference on Civil Society, June 2006.

20. See Mary Jo Bane, "The Context for Welfare Reform," *Welfare Realities: From Rhetoric to Reform* (Cambridge, MA: Harvard University Press, 1994).

21. Evelyn Z. Brodkin, "Inside the Welfare Conract: Discretion and Accountability in State Welfare Administration," *Social Science Review* (March 1997).

22. David T. Ellwood, *Poor Support: Poverty in the American Family* (New York: Basic Books, 1988), 237.

23. "Report to the Chairman, Subcommittee on Human Resources, Committee on Government Reform and Oversight, House of Representatives," October 1997, GAO/ HEHA 98-6.

24. William P. Ryan, "The New Landscape for Nonprofits," *Harvard Business Review* (January–February 1999).

25. Interview with Peter Cove.

26. "Temporary Assistance for Needy Families," Fourth Annual Report to Congress, April 2002, at www.acf.dhhs.gov.

27. J. Peterson and C. Nord, "The Regular Receipt of Child Support: A

Multi-Step Process," 102 (Washington, DC: US Department of Commerce, Bureau of the Census).

28. Chien-Chung Huang, Irwin Garfinkel, and Jane Waldfogel, "Child Support Enforcement and Welfare Caseloads," *Journal of Human Resources* 39, 1 (Winter 2004): 108.

29. "Child Support Fix Advances in Illinois Legislature," *Knight Ridder Tribune Business News,* April 14, 2003, 1.

30. Nadya Labi, "Deadbeat Profiteers," *Time,* September 2, 2002, 43.

31. "A Guide to Developing Public-Private Partnerships in Child Support" at www.acf.hhs.gov/progrmas/cse/rpt/pvt/contents/htm.

32. Ibid.

33. "Child Support Enforcement: States' Experiences with Private Agencies' Collection of Support Payments," GAO/HEHS-97-11.

34. "Augusta, Ga., Couple Run Business That Tracks Down Child Support," *Knight Ridder Tribune News Service,* April 23, 2004.

35. "Child Support Collection Falls Short, Lockheed Unit Won't Meet $80M First-Year Goal," *Daily Record* (Baltimore), December 3, 1997.

36. "The Ecology of Warning: How the Organizational Environment Affects Strategic Intelligence. Warning Report: New Warning Lenses Needed" (Report sponsored by the Global Futures Partnership, Sherman Kent School, CIA Directorate of Intelligence, June 17, 2002), 4–5.

37. Bruce D. Berkowitz and Allan E. Goodman, *Best Truth: Intelligence in the Information Age* (New Haven, CT: Yale University Press, 2000), 151.

38. Shane Ham and Robert D. Atkinson, "Modernizing the State Identification System: An Action Agenda," *Progressive Policy Institute Policy Report* (Washington, DC: Progressive Policy Institute, February 2002).

39. Ibid., 1.

40. Ibid., 6.

41. "FBI Promises to share more information with local law enforcement," at www.govexec.com. "Officials Say U.S. should have Shared Tip," *New York Times,* March 5, 2002, A11.

42. Laurie Garrett, "The Nightmare of Bioterrorism," *Foreign Affairs* 80, 1 (January/February 2001).

43. Terrence Kelly, "An Organizational Framework for Homeland Defense," *Parameters* (Carlisle Barracks, PA: Autumn 2001).

44. Tara O'Toole, Michael Mair, and Thomas V. Inglesby, "Shining Light on 'Dark Winter': Confronting Biological Weapons," *Clinical Infectious Diseases* 34 (April, 2002): 972–983.

45. Ibid., 982.

46. "Another Autumn: A Top Cop Won Fame and Blame for Profiling in the 1970s—New Terrorist Hunt Recalls 'Red Army' Campaign, Bitter Debate on Privacy—the Fears of 'Glass People,'" *Wall Street Journal,* December 10, 2001, A1.

47. "Senate Votes to Curb Project to Search for Terrorists in Databases and Internet Mail," *New York Times,* January 23, 2003.

48. "Cyber Crime Bleeds U.S. Corporations, Survey Shows; Financial Losses from Attacks Climb for Third Year in a Row" (Press release, Cyber Security Institute, San Francisco, April 7, 2002).

49. "10th CSI/FBI Survey Shows Cybercrime Losses Down for Fourth Straight Year" (Press release, Computer Security Institute, July 14, 2005).

50. "New Economy," *New York Times*, December 3, 2001.

51. Gov.exec.daily.com, October 31, 2002.

52. "Government, Industry Debate International IT Security Center," *Government Executive Daily Briefing,* October 28, 2002.

53. William B. Bonvillian and Kendra V. Sharp, "Homeland Security Technology," *Issues in Science and Technology Online* (Winter 2001) at http://www.issues.org/issues/18.2/bonvillian.html.

54. Ibid.

55. See, for instance, Joseph A. Barbera, Anthony G. Macintyre, and Craig A. DeAtley, "Ambulances to Nowhere: America's Critical Shortfall in Medical Preparedness for Catastrophic Terrorism" (Discussion Paper 2001-15 of the Belfer Center for Science and International Affairs, Kennedy School of Government, Harvard University, October 2001).

56. Remarks by Dr. Meselsen at "Undermining Terrorism," a conference at the John F. Kennedy School of Government, May 3, 2002.

57. Testimony of Senator Sam Nunn before the House Government Reform Committee Subcommittee on National Security, Veterans Affairs and International Relations, July 23, 2001.

58. See, for instance, Mark T. Imperial, "Collaboration and Performance Management in Network Settings: Lessons from Three Watershed Governance Efforts" (Washington, DC: IBM Center for The Business of Government, April 2004).

7

Government by Market

REINVENTED GOVERNMENT AND government by network are different from bureaucratic government and yet they each involve a significant amount of government as we know it. In reinvented organizations the public's work is done by people who work for the government; in government by network much of the public's work is paid for by the government even though it is not performed by people who work for the government and who, therefore, are not constrained by all of government's protocols and central-control mechanisms. In the third emerging model, government by market, the work of government involves few, if any, public employees and no public money. In government by market, the government uses state power to create a market that fulfills a public purpose. Often this involves taking into account what economists call "externalities."

I use the term "government by market" differently than have other scholars. For instance, B. Guy Peters uses market government to describe "the basic belief in the virtues of competition and an idealized pattern of exchange and incentives."[1] Most other public-administration scholars, when they talk about markets and government, are usually talking about what I have referred to previously as reinvented public-sector organizations or government by network in which market-style incentives are injected into systems run, either totally or mostly, with public money.

But government *by* market is something very distinctive. If reinvented government is government all dressed up to look like the private sector and government by network is government that hides behind much more popular organizations, government by market is so well disguised that most people are not even aware that it is government in operation. Because of this it is the model furthest from traditional bureaucratic government.

As discussed in Chapter 2, government by market, when applied to certain environmental problems, has been a big success. But only recently has this approach become politically acceptable. Rob Stavins, one of the early advocates of this approach in the environmental field, recalls how, just a decade ago, environmentalists chafed at the notion that you could buy and sell pollution. Behind their reaction and that of their colleagues in the government at the Environmental Protection Agency (EPA) was the feeling that using a market to control pollution was somehow immoral because the state was allowing polluters to pay for the right to pollute. That reaction, reports Stavins, has changed dramatically in recent years. The most ardent environmentalists will admit to the attractiveness of government by market, and now people seek to apply it in places where it may well not work.[2] As we shall see, the recent effort to deregulate the electricity market in California is a perfect example of an attempt at government by market where so much went wrong that energy executive Barbara Kates-Garnik has called it "the perfect storm."[3]

Government by market has shaped the education reform debate as well as the environmental protection debate. In education, government by market would break the current state monopoly on the provision of education by giving parents vouchers to purchase education wherever they want. But in this policy area government by market has failed to make much headway. The voucher movement argues that the government can create a market in education by attaching education money to each student instead of attaching education money to public schools. Those in the movement assert that government should use tax cuts and universal tuition tax credits to turn over education purchasing power to individuals—a vibrant education marketplace would result and offer consumers a range of services and products that the current system does not.

A vibrant market already exists in education at the college level where parents save, borrow, and do without in order to send children to elite, expensive, private institutions. And in recent years, as unhappiness with the public K–12 education system has grown, an education market of a sort has emerged even without government subsidies. Among others, Edison schools, Bright Horizons, and Nobel Learning Communities, which began as child-care providers and expanded business to include K-12 education, have created a new class of educators called "edupreneurs." The advantages of creating a market in education are many: to name a few, there are variety in curriculum; innovation in instruction methods; higher academic standards; weeding out substandard schools; introduction of new technologies in the classroom; and investments in research.

A recent US Supreme Court decision should help advocates of education vouchers but the vast majority of children still attend public schools run by traditional bureaucracies, and ballot proposals to extend the concept beyond some small experiments have generally failed. To understand when government by market succeeds and when it fails we must first understand some of its characteristics.

Characteristics of Government by Market

A well-functioning market is of course a marvel to behold. In our lifetimes it has given the vast majority of Americans color television, microwave ovens, and digital video disc players at prices that the vast majority of consumers can afford. And who knows what it will bring in the next century? But what is key here is "well-functioning." For those who attempt to design markets for public instead of private good the problems are immense. When government by market is effective the market is designed with the following characteristics:

- The price is right.
- The market is comprehensive (i.e., critical levels are not exempt from market forces).
- The rule of law exists and law enforcement is effective.
- Information about the market is of high quality and accessible to all who need it.

Policymakers attempting to design a market for public good must first get the price right. In Chapter 2 the market in used bottles and soft drink cans was discussed as a simple example of government by market. In the creation of those markets, too high a price on bottles would clearly have wrecked much of the beverage industry and caused a serious outcry from the public. (To this day the beer industry remains opposed to bottle bills wherever they have not yet taken root.) Too low a price on bottles would not have solved the litter problem at all. Similarly, if the number of pollution permits is so high that they cost very little to buy, they will not create an incentive for energy plants to clean up their manufacturing. If the number of permits is too low, however, the price would be so high that older plants would go out of business.

One of the reasons that voucher systems for education have not been very successful is that they attempt to introduce vouchers into school districts while preserving the public education system. This means that, instead of taking the full price of educating a child (which in some jurisdictions can be as high as $ 8,000 to $12,000) and giving that amount of money to parents in the form of a voucher, most voucher plans give only a fraction of the money (usually around $2,500) to parents. The result is that the amount of money per child is not really enough to create a vibrant and competitive market because the older, monopolistic system has been allowed to stand. Not surprisingly, in those cities where voucher systems have come into existence, it is often church schools (mostly Roman Catholic) with other sources of income that jump to take in the students with vouchers.

A second example of policymakers' attempting to introduce the rigor of the market into public policy is the Medicare+Choice program started in the late 1990s. Medicare is a classic example of government by network in that government picks up the entire cost of health care for the elderly. The care is provided by a wide variety of private, for-profit, and nonprofit providers. Thinking that health maintenance organizations (HMOs) would offer better, more efficient services, the Medicare+Choice program sought to get seniors to sign up for HMOs instead of the traditional fee-for-service programs. HMOs would offer such services as prescription drug coverage and save money for the government at the same time because HMOs would try to compete to cover Medicare patients.

This attempt to inject market forces into a government program might have worked, but in classic fashion the government essentially got the price wrong. "The Medicare+Choice program promised too much. It promised cuts to taxpayers, richer benefits to Medicare recipients and a slice of the pie for HMO companies. An agenda like that was too good to be true."[4] In 1999 HMOs started pulling out of the Medicare market. Between 1999 and 2003 HMOs and other private plans dropped 2.4 million Medicare patients from their plans—mostly because the government was reimbursing the private plans by increasing their payments 2 percent a year, while costs were rising at closer to 10 percent a year.[5] When Congress passed a Medicare prescription-drug program in the summer of 2003, the HMOs that were left in the business expected that some financial help would be on the way and the flood of companies out of the market slowed.

For decades, reformers have felt that the injection of forces for competition into the Medicare program could help forestall the fiscal crisis that now looms as a result of the coming baby boomers' retirements. This may still be right, but in government-provided health care programs at least, the desire to save money has meant that the "price" set by the government has been wrong. Without accurate pricing, there is no way that government can get the requisite efficiencies from a market that, like the Medicare+Choice market, will fail before the efficiencies are ever realized.

The new prescription-drug benefit, added to Medicare in the first term of the Bush administration, is further proof that injecting markets into systems that are not really markets produces confusion and implementation failures. The pricing may be right, given that the costs of the program are significantly higher than predicted at its passage. But the attempt to inject more market mechanisms into a system that is not a market has produced a plan that is confusing and frustrating to the "customers"—elderly people who must now figure out how the program works.[6]

Second, policymakers who decide to try to use government by market must have the courage of their convictions and establish a comprehensive market that does not leave any segments immune from market pressures. When California politicians decided to deregulate the energy market in 1996, they expected that government by market would create a situation where power bills to the state's biggest users would be cut, and thus spur economic growth. In the first few years things went well, but by the summer of 2000 it was clear that instead of creating a well-functioning market California lawmakers had created a nightmare. The state experienced soaring prices, cities and counties suffered from blackouts, and consumers had to pay higher prices.

The story of the California energy crisis, which is still being written, is a story of an unsuccessful effort in government by market. In the words of a *Wall Street Journal* report: "Government created a complex market ripe for manipulation. Growing demand and tight supplies let energy sellers dictate—and in some cases manipulate—prices, unchecked by half-hearted and overmatched regulators."[7]

In an effort to buy political support for the venture, the designers of this market controlled prices to consumers by cutting them 10 percent and then freezing prices for five years. This was all well and good while real prices were falling but a disaster when they began to rise. In addition, the designers of the market created not one market but three: a day-ahead market, a reserve market, and a real-time market. The three markets, plus such features of the plan as high payments for alleviating congestion, created many opportunities for arbitrage. The complexity of the market and the opportunities for arbitrage were combined with weak regulatory authorities that, apparently, allowed companies like Enron and others to manipulate the market, force prices up, and generally contribute to (or even cause) the crisis. But whether the crisis was the result of illegal actions by energy traders or traders taking advantage of opportunities for arbitrage, the lesson for those who would create a market to do the public's business is the same—design matters.[8]

Third, using government by market to achieve a public good presupposes a certain amount of honesty in the economic system and a certain level of honesty and effectiveness in law enforcement. Although market government applied to environmental problems has proven a success in the United States, it is not surprising that talk here about creating "market mechanisms" to implement the Kyoto Accords falls on skeptical ears in other countries. Market government works where the rule of law is well established and where law enforcement is effective enough to deter cheating (or frequently catch it and prosecute it). This is simply not the case in much of the world.

Finally, the importance of a well-established rule of law in order to use government by market is mandatory for government by market. A well-functioning market depends on high-quality information and universal access to it. An important trend in government regulation is known as "information-based regulation." In information-based regulation the role of the state is minimal; it simply passes a law requiring the disclosure of certain kinds of information. The most famous, and still one of the most effective examples, is the Toxic Release Inventory (TRI) established in 1988. It requires that more than 21,000 US facilities report the release of hundreds of toxic chemicals to the EPA which then publishes them. Even though government action in information-based regulation is minimal, what the TRI and other disclosure laws (e.g., the Home Mortgage Disclosure Act) accomplish is far from minimal. Archon Fong writes:

> Journalists, investors, environmental activists, and citizens can easily use TRI to construct blacklists that shame intensive polluters and mobilize campaigns against them. In response to this pressure or to avoid it, many plant managers have pursued reduction and prevention measures. Between 1988 and 1997, for example, total release of toxic chemicals tracked by TRI declined to 49% nationwide...[9]

In any well-developed democracy with a vibrant civil society and an established rule of law, simple disclosure can be enough to induce behavior that is in the public interest by those who would like to avoid public censure—not to mention lawsuits. In fact, public disclosure works especially well in the United States, where a very litigious population can be counted on to make use of information about pollution or other possibly harmful practices. Public disclosure and government by market is not likely to work, however, in many places that do not share these traditions.

The utility of information in a government by market setting is only as good as the information itself. For instance, it is not surprising that there has been substantial opposition to education voucher plans from teachers unions, school administrators, and other members of the pubic education monopoly. But parents and others with no professional stake in the status quo have been almost as reluctant to embrace the market approach to education. Lurking behind the failure of so many voucher plans is the suspicion that somehow, someone will be taken for a ride. Buying a second-grade education is simply not as easy as buying a bread-making machine. There are many sources of information about bread-making machines, cars, and other consumer products, and most Americans know how to find them and understand them. But sources of information about one school's second grade versus another school's are hard to come by and difficult to interpret. Good markets require good information, and, in spite of the recent trend toward testing, good information is simply not so easy to come by for most parents.

Problems aside, however, government by market is a very powerful alternative to bureaucratic government precisely because it allows an unlimited number of individual adaptations to achieve the overall public good. In reinvented public-sector organizations, government is the one entity pursuing the public good; in government by network, government is the one entity choosing a finite number of organizations to pursue the public good. In contrast, government by market allows individuals (as in the case of what to do with bottles) or companies (as in the case of how to limit sulfur dioxide emissions) to pursue the public good as they see fit. It is, therefore, perfectly suited to this country, where citizens value individual choice and chafe at any system that feels as if it is too controlling.

Increasingly, modern society finds itself having to cope with problems that reinvented government or even government by network cannot solve. At that point leaders have to begin to create markets for the public good. Consider the case of garbage. Governments deal with many big and important issues, one of them being the production and disposal of garbage. It is one of the basic functions of local government and it is crucial to public health. Most localities started out collecting garbage and bringing it to landfills. As the landfills became too full, people began to oppose them for health reasons and argue for closing them; new landfills were no longer wanted near residential neighborhoods. In the meantime the environmental movement taught most Americans the value of recycling. We are running out of places to put our garbage, and many cities, stuck in old bureaucratic paradigms, are trying to figure out what to do next.

Over the past decade there has been a shift away from public management of garbage and toward more participation of the private sector. Most of these forms are manifested in classic government by network, in which local government contracts with a variety of companies for waste disposal. In 1994 between 40 and 50 percent of garbage collection in the United States was owned and operated by the private sector; by the end of the decade that number was closer to 68 percent, and was predicted to be over 70 percent by 2005.[10]

But even government by network, which has worked to reduce costs for many localities, will not be sufficient to cope with the fact that cities are drowning in trash and that with every passing year they have fewer and fewer places to put it. Take the case of New York City, which generates enormous amounts of trash in a very small area. The outstanding example of New York City's ongoing garbage disposal problems is still found in the Mobro 4000 incident of 1987. Mobro was a garbage barge from Long Island that sailed around in the Atlantic Ocean and into the Caribbean looking for a place to deposit that collection of the city's garbage. The story made national headlines as one community after another refused to accept the barge's cargo, even though there was no hazardous waste, as rumored. The reason it had nowhere to unload the garbage originated with plain old corruption: New York City's waste management bureaucracy had always had an interesting relationship with organized crime. In the instance of Mobro, an inexperienced barge owner made a deal with a crime boss and accepted the garbage without a disposal agreement. According to Kojo N. Oduro, a former Kennedy School student who reminded me of this story, the boss is now in jail for conspiring to murder other trash haulers. The point about the Mobro fiasco is not only the wake-up call for the city, but a reminder to the world about potential landfill crises and the principles involved in the export of municipal waste material.[11]

In the years since Mobro, New York City's trash problem has not eased. The city's recycling program has been run in classic bureaucratic fashion with lots of rules and frequent rule changes, a not uncommon reaction to corruption in government services. Garbage collectors in New York City are unionized and make healthy salaries, but the system continues as an old-fashioned, rule-driven bureaucracy. One instance alone shows this: in the summer of 2003, *armed* sanitation police could be found going through trash containers looking for recyling violations.[12]

Armed recycling police? It sounds ridiculous, but that is what happens when a government sticks to the bureaucratic model. And New York's recycling program came to be such a mess that Mayor Michael Bloomberg stopped it for a year to reevaluate it. Like other communities, this city still faces big garbage disposal and recycling problems. Landfills are full, and very few other countries want other people's garbage under any circumstances.

The eventual solution to the crisis is not to privatize collection but to get people to produce less garbage. Contracting out the collection of garbage may get rid of some of New York City's problems but it will not solve the fundamental problem. The only way to do that is through government by market—and the mechanism is pretty simple. Charge people for garbage pickup, but charge less for smaller amounts to be collected. In San Francisco, citizens who reduce their garbage amount from 32 to 20 gallons (volume measure) pay less for collection. The city allows collection by private companies and has brought its recycling rate up from 46 to 52 percent in 2002, while New York is still struggling to achieve a 12 percent rate.[13] In Portland, Oregon, all garbage collection billing is based on the amount of garbage generated. A small roll cart is $19.95 per week, a 60-gallon roll cart is $24.65, and a 90-gallon roll cart is $28.55.[14] By April 2001 Portland was recovering 54 percent of its residential and commercial waste.[15]

These differences cannot be attributed to a greater desire to be environmentally conscious in San Francisco or Portland than in New York. All three cities are heavily Democratic cities. Citizens in all these cities are to the left of center among those in the United States and express a high regard for environmental values. The difference is that San Francisco's and Portland's governments have created an effective market, quite in contrast to the situation in New York City.

Government by market is the least used and consequently the least understood of the three new modes of policy implementation discussed in this book. But as the garbage example shows, sometimes policy problems cannot be solved with any of the more traditional forms of governance. We turn now to more examples of how government by market can be applied to the two policy areas in this book.

Preventing Welfare
Dependence and Sustaining Independence

Child-Care Vouchers. The goal of modern welfare policy has been to create a system that moves people from dependence toward self-sufficiency by creating a system that rewards work. As the old welfare system moved out from under the stifling effects of the traditional bureaucracy, it reinvented and reengineered eligibility and it created a network through which to deliver the critical support and training needed to move welfare recipients into work. But the transformation of the welfare system has also been aided by major reforms in two areas critical to keeping women off welfare—child care and taxes—both of which are examples of government by market.

One of the most important insights of the welfare reformers of the 1980s and 1990s was that women on welfare often got jobs but lost them quickly because of the difficulties they encountered paying for and keeping good child care. Expanded access to child care was one of the most important reasons that the welfare reforms of the 1990s could finally move the system to a work-based system. Subsidizing child care is so important to keeping mothers in the workplace, as one study found: "Reforms that reduce social assistance payments concurrently with improving child care subsidies, for instance, have the strongest positive effects on employment of low income mothers."[16]

Thus a system that effectively subsidizes child care is critical to keeping women in the workforce, and, not surprisingly, the welfare reforms of 1996 included significant increases in the amounts of money available to welfare mothers for child care. In deciding how to implement this system, however, the reformers faced several choices. They could attempt the traditional bureaucratic response: create a string of government-run day-care centers. But by the 1990s this example of the bureaucratic instinct was judged as so obsolete that it was not even discussed as an option. A second way was to contract with day-care centers to take care of children of welfare clients, an example of government by network. But this would mean a limited number of centers exclusively for welfare families, and would have forced families into one model of day care.

Instead, the framers chose the simplest and most flexible option—making day-care vouchers or certificates available to parents who qualified and allow their use at any licensed facility. Through the use of vouchers government was creating a market for people who had been left out of the mainstream, middle-class child-care market. The chief advantage of the market being provided was to allow parents a variety of choices. In its report to Congress, the Administration for Children and Families of HHS, which distributes the relevant block grant, emphasizes that parents can "select any legally operating child-care provider—including child care centers, family members, neighbors, family child care homes, after-school programs and faith-based programs."[17]

The choices inherent in this market have made it very popular—so popular that in spite of a $4.8 billion appropriation in 2004 demand exceeds supply. In Massachusetts, for example, the state pays a range between the thirtieth and forty-fifth percentile of market rate, which means that there are simply not enough slots at the subsidized rate to go around.[18] All the same, the approach of government by market to child care is likely to be the preferred way for the foreseeable future.

The Earned Income Tax Credit. One of the most important antipoverty programs of the past decade and one whose contribution to shrinking welfare rolls cannot be dismissed is the earned income tax credit. Its historical antecedents, the negative income tax and Richard Nixon's Family Assistance Program (FAP), failed because politicians feared, with some justification, that these programs would be even more expensive than the then-current welfare system and that they would provide even less incentive to work. In fairly blunt language, Senator Russell Long told President Nixon that his committee objected to "paying people not to work" and to "lay about all day making love and producing illegitimate babies."[19]

Long had a better idea—one that was to receive increasing support as disenchantment with the welfare bureaucracy grew. This was an alternative to the FAP that directed tax benefits to the "deserving poor" (that is, those who worked). When it finally passed in 1975 it "embodied Long's vision of a program that moved individuals off welfare and into paid employment, while keeping others off the welfare rolls. It covered only working poor families with children, and forced the 'undeserving poor' either to choose paid employment or resort to stigmatized and inadequate AFDC services."[20]

In spite of the political popularity of the earned income tax credit, it was not until the late 1980s and the 1990s that the program became as robust a part of the fight against welfare dependence as it is today. Because the program had not been adjusted since its enactment it had lost some of its value in real terms. Thus the first big increase of the program came as part of the tax reforms of 1986, which increased the maximum benefit, increased the level at which the benefit was to be phased out, and, perhaps most important to the long-run efficacy of the program, indexed it to inflation. But the really big increases in the program came in 1993 when amendments extended the credit to those who had no children and raised the phase-out point once again. In the ten years between 1986 and 1996 the cost of the credit increased by 1,191 percent.[21]

Although expansion of the credit had begun under the first President Bush, its expansion under President Clinton was an important part of his pledge to "change welfare as we know it." As states were implementing time limits on welfare and making sure that welfare recipients worked, the expanded earned income tax credit offset much of the tax burden on low-income workers—especially the payroll tax, which affects low-income workers the most.

The credit has proven to be the powerhouse of antipoverty pro-

Table 7.1   Using Government by Market to Reduce Welfare Dependence

	Eligibility	Transition to Work	Preventing and Sustaining Independence
Government by market			Vouchers for child care
			The earned income tax credit

grams, increasing labor-force participation among single workers (something the bureaucratic welfare system repeatedly failed to do) and lifting more children out of poverty than any other government program.[22] The credit was "transformed from an obscure tax credit to a more visible social instrument with significant anti-poverty responsibilities."[23]

Day-care vouchers and the earned income tax credit are good examples of policymakers deciding to move away from bureaucratic government and look to the creation of a market. In the case of day-care vouchers, policymakers understood the diversity of both the market and the choices that most parents desire. Thus a portable voucher allows those who qualify entrance to the day-care market. The credit uses the tax system to increase the value of low-paying jobs. It does not put the government in the position of trying to create jobs for poor people, a strategy that remained attractive to some in the policy world until recently. Nor does it try to limit the employment choices of poor people to companies that receive subsidies. It allows the low-income labor market to work but increases the value of wages in that market in order to keep people out of the welfare system.

Table 7.1 summarizes some of the ways that government by market contributes to the fight for self-sufficiency among the previously welfare dependent.

Applying Government by Market to the Problem of Homeland Security

Of all the models of government in the twenty-first century discussed in this book, government by market is perhaps the most powerful model and the most difficult to use. In the case of the earned income tax credit, it took nearly two decades before its potential as a tool to use against poverty and welfare dependence was implemented. Government by market is powerful because it allows for infinite innovation in accomplishing the public goals. But it does require, at the outset, the political will to establish the goal in the first place. That will existed in the efforts to move out of a failed welfare bureaucratic state—it does not yet exist in some of the areas that might make the most important contributions to homeland security. But if it should, government by market will prove an equally powerful tool.

Applying Government by Market to Reducing Dependence on Fossil Fuels

For some decades now, US presidents have given mostly lip service to the goal of reducing our dependence on fossil fuels. The most recent addition to this long line was President Bush, who stated in his 2006 state of the union address that it was time to break the nation's "addiction" to fossil fuels. It was quickly noted, however, that this rhetoric had not been matched, in the Bush administration or any others, by a serious program of action.

But at some point rhetoric may cross over to action. After all, Americans have fought two wars in the Middle East and they confront daily growing evidence of the effect of fossil fuels on global warming. Our cautious relations with Saudi Arabia (home of the vast majority of the September 11 hijackers and funding source of much of Al-Qaeda) have been shaped by our appetite for its oil. At some point, we as a nation may come to the conclusion that over the years we have paid too high a price for our dependence on foreign oil. Putting aside for a moment the serious environmental consequences of increasing domestic production to replace oil imports, increasing such production when there is a finite amount of domestic oil is simply not a decent long-term solution. At some point, whether for environmental or foreign policy reasons or both, we may want to get serious about weaning our economy from fossil fuels.

Here is where government by market comes in. To wean the economy from fossil fuels without wrecking it, the government will have to create a sophisticated market that subsidizes the use of alternative energy sources and discourages the use of fossil fuels until technological progress moves us away from fossil fuels altogether. Market thinking on this question has not been limited to one end of the political spectrum. People from both ends of the political spectrum (e.g., former vice president Al Gore, conservative economist Martin Feldstein) have been thinking in terms of government by market.

In the summer of his 2000 presidential campaign, Al Gore proposed an energy plan that consisted of a series of tax incentives for the use of nonfossil fuels. These incentives, the largest of which was a tax credit for the purchase of new automobiles using hybrid fuels, were intended to stimulate the market in alternative energy. The tax credits were also intended to be phased out over a period of ten years. Martin Feldstein has proposed a system of tradable oil conservation vouchers modeled on the successful experiment with tradable permits to reduce sulfur dioxide emissions.[24] The vouchers could be traded among households, encouraging the use of public transportation and fuel-efficient cars for those seeking to sell their vouchers and creating an extra cost for those wanting to continue to drive vehicles with high fuel consumption.

The advantage of government by market is that it would allow for millions of adaptations and would encourage dramatic increases in innovation—if the government has the will to set the reduction of fossil fuel use as a serious national goal. Here the disadvantage of traditional government is obvious. Americans have no desire to live in a state where a giant bureaucracy polices their consumption of energy, so in this very important policy area government by market is the only implementation option.

Applying Government by Market to Research on Drugs to Counter Biological Terrorism Effects

Government by market is a very efficient way of stimulating innovation. Right now, as Bonvillian and Sharp point out, in regard to our response to biological terrorism there is "zero market incentive to develop effective vaccines or treatments for bio-terror attacks."[25] We will need to develop new drugs and explore the use of existing drugs in response to a wide variety of biochemical terrorism agents. While research grants and other government-led activities may accomplish some of this, in the long run we must enlist the research capacities of the entire pharmaceutical industry.

How? There are plenty of market incentives to develop drugs for breast cancer or the common cold, but there are precious few to develop drugs for diseases like smallpox or Ebola that may never be used. Thus the government needs to explore the creation of market incentives that would encourage the pharmaceutical industry to devote at least some research to this problem. There are many possible options, from tax breaks to patent extensions, that could be put together to create a market where none currently exists.

Table 7.2 presents some examples of how government by market can achieve homeland security missions.

Table 7.2   **Using Government by Market to Achieve Homeland-Security Missions (Examples)**

	Prevention	Protection	Response
Government by market	Create markets that reduce dependence on fossil fuels in order to make the nation less dependent on foreign oil		Create economic incentives for research into vaccines or treatments against biological terrorism threats

Conclusion

Government by market is a powerful new mode of policy implementation, but it is one about which we know very little. For every example of the government having created a market to achieve a public good (e.g., reducing SO_2 pollution or increasing recycling), we have examples of the creation of a market failing to live up to its expectations in, for example, education, health care, and energy. The successes and failures should be studied, for by doing so we shall learn how and where to use this powerful new tool.

One final word on government by market is that it only works when there is true consensus on the policy outcome, and that is a matter of politics—not policy implementation. It worked, for example, when a consensus emerged seeking to reduce a harmful substance such as SO_2. On the other hand, the failure to fully implement the Kyoto Accords is but one example of how long it takes to create a consensus on a policy issue.

Notes

1. B. Guy Peters, *The Future of Governing: Four Emerging Models,* (Lawrence: University Press of Kansas, 1996), 22.

2. Interview with the author on June 21, 2000.

3. Interview with the author on April 20, 1999.

4. "Don't let Medicare+Choice Program Fail," *San Francisco Chronicle,* August 15, 2000.

5. "Fewer People on Medicare Are Dropped by HMO's," *New York Times,* September 9, 2003.

6. "Rival Visions Led to Rocky Start for Drug Benefit," *New York Times,* February 6, 2006.

7. "As California Starved for Energy, U.S. Businesses Had a Feast," *Wall Street Journal,* September 16, 2002.

8. Jerry Taylor and Peter VanDoren, "Did Enron Pillage California?" (Cato Institute Briefing Paper 72, Washington, DC, August 22, 2002).

9. "Smart Regulation: How Government is Marshalling Firms and Citizens to Protect the Environment" (Taubman Center Report, Harvard University, 2000).

10. "Public Works: Service Delivery Choices: Special Data Issue" (International City County Management Association, Washington, DC, 1994). See also "1997 Trends in Solid-Waste Recycling Privatization," at www. privatization.org/databas/policyissues/solidwaste_1997trends.html.

11. Kojo N. Oduro, "Recyling of Waste in New York City as Seen through the Lens of the Principles of C21st Government" (Paper prepared for API 416, January 2004).

12. Ibid. Reported in Oduro at www.junipercivic.com.

13. Ibid., 24. See also San Francisco Chronicle, December 12, 2002.

14. See "City of Portland Solid Waste and Recycling Rates And Charges Effective August 1, 2004," www.portland.or.gov.

15. Ibid.

16. Gordon Cleveland and Douglas Hyatt, "Child Care Subsidies, Welfare Reforms and Loan Mothers," Industrial Relations 42, 3 (April 2003): 251.

17. "Child Care and Development Fund Report to Congress—Fiscal Year 2001," Administration for Children and Families at http://nccic.acf.hhs.gov/.

18. "The Dilemmas of Day Care: Too Few State Subsidies Leave Struggling Families Searching for Answers," Telegram and Gazette (Worcester, MA), August 20, 2004.

19. Quoted in Dennis J. Ventry Jr., "The Collision of Tax and Welfare Politics: The Political History of the Earned Income Tax Credit, 1969–1999," National Tax Journal 53, 4, Pt. 2 (December, 2000): 992.

20. Ibid., 995.

21. Ibid., 1005.

22. Ibid., 1011.

23. Ibid., 1016.

24. Martin Feldstein, "Oil Dependence and National Security: A Market-based System for Reducing U.S. Vulnerability," National Interest (Fall 2001).

25. "Homeland Security Technology," Issues in Science and Technology 18, 22 (2002): 43–49.

8

Leadership in Twenty-First-Century Government

THE PRESIDENT OF the United States in the year 2050 may still live in the city of Washington, DC, but the city may have turned many of the huge buildings of the old government into parks or movie theaters. Nevertheless, the absence of buildings and the absence of quite so many bureaucrats will not necessarily mean that government is dead. In fact, it might mean that government is smaller and cheaper but simultaneously better at doing what people want it to do.

If we are conscious about what is happening to government, we can make it happen better. If we are not, we can proceed to waste a great deal of money and fail a great many people. Reinvented government can be as costly and as wasteful as the old government it is trying to dress up. Government by network can turn into thousands of contracting horror stories and millions of wasted dollars if it is not managed correctly and if the political will to hold organizations in the network accountable is lacking. Government by market can be manipulated and the source of many unintended consequences if the market is not designed right and enforced properly.

For the complex array of reasons laid out in Chapter 1, policymakers are likely to remain interested in alternatives to the traditional bureaucratic state as they seek to implement policy. The first challenge they will face is to understand that they have implementation options. The second challenge will be to match policy goals with the appropriate implementation model. And the third challenge will be to hold these new forms of government accountable while preserving the capacity for innovation and adaptation.

Two final factors will shape the postbureaucratic state: the recruiting of talented and highly skilled government executives and the relationship between the executive and the legislative branch in the next century. All the new forms of government discussed in this book will result in smaller government, but they will also require better-paid and better-educated government officials. In recent years, in the United States and in some Western democracies government wages at the top of the wage scale have stagnated as private-sector wages at the top of the scale have exploded.[1] If the government is to remain an effective force, people need to be able to make nearly as much money in the public sector as in the private sector. Each of the new forms of government requires a sophisticated package of skills and a broad education—the kinds of skills and backgrounds often found among leaders of industry. Western democracies are fooling themselves if they think that they can manage into the next century without addressing the wage gap at the top between the public and the private sectors.

Second, Congress and legislative bodies in other countries will have to learn to carry out oversight of the new forms of government. A major role of Congress in recent decades has been to perform oversight of the bureaucracy, and there is some evidence that congressional oversight activities increased between the 1970s and the 1990s.[2] Much of the oversight that the public sees comes in the form of "fire alarm" oversight, investigations into large-scale problems in the conduct of the executive branch.[3]

Nonetheless, in spite of passing the GPRA Congress has largely ignored the revolution in government taking place within the executive branch. While the use of performance measures by appropriators has been increasing, there is scant evidence for Congress's exacting consequences for poor performance. OMB Circular 11, issued in 2003, does require that performance indicators and performance goals be included in the basic justification materials sent on to Congress. But, of the twenty-six "high-risk" programs on the GAO list nearly all are still in existence and being funded.[4]

There are a variety of reasons for this. First of all, in recent years Congress has largely ignored authorizing activity, a natural process in which to consider the pros and cons of implementation, in favor of an appropriations process that has become all-consuming. This trend has gotten so bad that Congress even appropriates money for programs it has not authorized.[5] The absence of systematic authorizing behavior not generated by an emergency has led many to advocate a biennial budget process to free more time for authorization and oversight. In a legislature consumed with appropriating at the expense of authorizing, there is simply no room for evaluation of existing bureaucratic structures, let alone evaluation of new implementation structures that require a higher level of oversight. Complicating this problem is the severe mismatch between the organization structures of the executive branch and the committee system of Congress. This mismatch leaves some important departments, such as EPA and DHS, reporting to tens of different committees.

The situation is similar in other advanced democracies. The revolution in executive government seems to have proceeded without the legislative branch. Jonathan Bruel, a former OMB official with close ties to the OECD says, "There is not much evidence in the world that money moves because of performance."[6]

Nonetheless, executive branch failure has enormous consequences for the civil servants and the politicians they report to—not to mention the citizens. The complexity of modern policy challenges will continue to drive innovations in the way policy is implemented. If the United States and the other advanced democracies can create new forms of government, secure the talent to lead them, and figure out how to hold these new forms accountable, democratic governments in the next century should be able to serve their citizens as well or better than they did in the past century.

Notes

1. George J. Borjas, "Wage Structures and the Sorting of Workers into the Public Sector," *For the People: Can We Fix Public Service?,* John D. Donahue and Joseph S. Nye Jr., eds. (Washington, DC: Brookings Institution Press, 2003).

2. Joel D. Aberbach, *Keeping a Watchful Eye: The Politics of Congressional Oversight,* (Washington, DC: Brookings Institution Press, 1990).

3. Matthew D. McCubbins and Thomas Schwartz, "Congressional Oversight Overlooked: Police Patrols versus Fire Alarms," *American Journal of Political Science* 28 (1984): 165–179.

4. Virginia L. Thomas, "Restoring Government Integrity Through Performance, Results and Accountability," *Policy Research and Analysis* (Washington, DC: Heritage Foundation, June 26, 2000).

5. Ibid.

6. Conversation between the author and Jonathan Bruel, July 10, 2006.

Selected Bibliography

Anechiarico, Frank, and James B. Jacobs. *The Pursuit of Absolute Integrity: How Corruption Control Makes Government Ineffective.* Chicago: University of Chicago Press, 1996.

Bane, Mary Jo, and David T. Ellwood. *Welfare Realities: From Welfare to Reform.* Cambridge, MA: Harvard University Press, 1994.

Barzelay, Michael. *Breaking Through Bureaucracy.* Berkeley: University of California Press, 1992.

Behn, Bob. *Rethinking Democratic Accountability.* Washington, DC: Brookings Institution Press, 2001.

Berkowitz, Bruce D., and Allan E. Goodman. *Best Truth: Intelligence in the Information Age.* New Haven, CT: Yale University Press, 2000.

Bognador, Vernon. *Joined Up Government.* Oxford: Oxford University Press, 2005.

Boston, Jonathan, John Martin, June Pallot, and Pat Walsh. *Public Management, the New Zealand Model.* Auckland: Oxford University Press, 1996.

"Ecology of Warning: How the Organizational Environment Affects Strategic Intelligence. Warning Report: New Warning Lenses Needed." Report sponsored by the Global Futures Partnership, Sherman Kent School, CIA Directorate of Intelligence, June 17, 2002.

Ellwood, David T. *Poor Support: Poverty in the American Family.* New York: Basic Books, 1988.

Feldstein, Martin. "Oil Dependence and National Security: A Market-based System for Reducing U.S. Vulnerability." *The National Interest* (Fall 2001).

Fountain, Jane. *Virtual Government.* Washington, DC: Brookings Institution Press, 2001.

Goldsmith, Stephen, and William D. Eggers. *Governing by Network: The New Shape of the Public Sector.* Washington, DC: Brookings Institution Press, 2004.

Gore, Al. *Creating a Government That Works Better and Costs Less: Report of the National Performance Review.* Washington, DC: Government Printing Office, September 1993.

———. *The Best Kept Secrets in Washington.* Washington, DC: Government Printing Office, 1996.

Kamarck, Elaine Ciulla. "The Globalization of Public Administration Reform." In *Governance in a Globalizing World,* edited by Joseph S. Nye Jr. and John D. Donahue. Washington, DC: Brookings Institution Press, 2000.

Kelman, Steve. "Strategic Contracting Management." In *Market Based Governance,* edited by John D. Donahue and Joseph S. Nye Jr. Washington, DC: Brookings Institution Press, 2002.

Light, Paul. *Monitoring Government: Inspectors General and the Search for Accountability.* Washington, DC: Brookings Institution Press, 1993.

Lipsky, Michael. *Street Level Bureaucracy.* New York: Russell Sage Foundation, 1983.

Lipsky, Michael, and Steven Smith. *Nonprofits for Hire: The Welfare State in the Age of Contracting.* Cambridge, MA: Harvard University Press, 1993.

Milward, H. Brinton, and Keith G. Provan. "Governing the Hollow State." *Journal of Public Administration Research and Theory* (April 2000).

Norris, Pippa, ed. *Critical Citizens: Global Support for Democratic Governance.* Oxford: Oxford University Press, 1999.

Nye, Joseph S. Jr., et al. *Why People Don't Trust Government.* Cambridge, MA: Harvard University Press, 1997.

Osborne, David. *Laboratories of Democracy.* Boston: Harvard Business School Press, 1988.

Osborne, David, and Peter Plastrick. *Banishing Bureaucracy: The Five Strategies for Reinventing Government.* Reading, MA: Addison-Wesley, 1997.

O'Toole, Laurence J., Jr. "The Implications for Democracy in a Networked Bureaucratic World." *Journal of Public Administration Research and Theory* 3 (July 1997).

Peters, B. Guy. *The Future of Governing: Four Emerging Models.* Lawrence: University Press of Kansas, 1993.

Pinkerton, James P. *What Comes Next: the End of Big Government and the New Paradigm Ahead.* New York: Hyperion Press, 1995.

Pressman, Jeffrey L., and Aaron B. Wildavsky. *Implementation: How Great Expectations in Washington are Dashed in Oakland.* Berkeley: University of California Press, 1973.

Salamon, Lester, ed. *The Tools of Government: A Guide to the New Governance.* Oxford: Oxford University Press, 2002.

Savoie, Donald S. *Thatcher, Reagan and Mulroney.* Pittsburg: University of Pittsburg Press, 1994.

Singer, Peter. *Corporate Warriors: The Rise of the Privatized Military Industry.* Ithaca, NY: Cornell University Press, 2003.

Stavins, Robert N. "What Can We Learn from the Grand Policy Experiment? Lessons from SO_2 Allowance Trading." *Journal of Economic Perspectives* 12, 3 (Summer 1998).

Stone, Robert. *Confessions of a Civil Servant: Lessons in Changing America's Government and Military.* Lanham, MD: Rowman & Littlefield, 2003.

UK Government's Approach to Public Service Reform: A Discussion Paper. London: Public Service Reform Team, 2006.

Index

About the Book

IN THE LAST decades of the twentieth century, many political leaders declared that government was, in the words of Ronald Reagan, "the problem, not the solution." But on closer inspection, argues Elaine Kamarck, the revolt against "government" was and is a revolt against bureaucracy—a revolt that has taken place in first world, developing, and avowedly communist countries alike.

To some, this looks like the end of government. Kamarck, however, counters that what we are seeing is the replacement of the traditional bureaucratic approach with new models more in keeping with the information age economy. *The End of Government* explores the emerging contours of this new, postbureaucratic state—the sequel to government as we know it—considering: What forms will it take? Will it work in all policy arenas? Will it serve democratic ideals more effectively than did the bureaucratic state of the previous century? Perhaps most significantly, how will leadership be redefined in these new circumstances?

Kamarck's provocative work makes it clear that, in addition to figuring out *what* to do, today's government leaders face an unprecedented number of options when it comes to *how* to do things. The challenge of government increasingly will be to choose an implementation mode, match it to a policy problem, and manage it well in the postbureaucratic world.

Elaine C. Kamarck is lecturer in public policy at Harvard University's John F. Kennedy School of Government. Previously, she was a senior policy adviser to the Clinton administration, where she ran the National Performance Review, and a political columnist for *Newsday* and the *Los Angeles Times*. She is coeditor, with Joseph S. Nye, Jr., of *Governance.com: Democracy in the Information Age.*